SECOND EDITION

Kubernetes Cookbook
Building Cloud Native Applications

Sameer Naik, Sébastien Goasguen,
and Jonathan Michaux

Beijing · Boston · Farnham · Sebastopol · Tokyo

Kubernetes Cookbook

by Sameer Naik, Sébastien Goasguen, and Jonathan Michaux

Published by O'Reilly Media, Inc., 1005 Gravenstein Highway North, Sebastopol, CA 95472.

O'Reilly books may be purchased for educational, business, or sales promotional use. Online editions are also available for most titles (*http://oreilly.com*). For more information, contact our corporate/institutional sales department: 800-998-9938 or *corporate@oreilly.com*.

Acquisitions Editor: John Devins	**Indexer:** Ellen Troutman-Zaig
Development Editor: Jeff Bleiel	**Interior Designer:** David Futato
Production Editor: Elizabeth Faerm	**Cover Designer:** Karen Montgomery
Copyeditor: Kim Wimpsett	**Illustrator:** Kate Dullea
Proofreader: Rachel Head	

March 2018:	First Edition
November 2023:	Second Edition

Revision History for the Second Edition
2023-11-13:   First Release

See *http://oreilly.com/catalog/errata.csp?isbn=9781098142247* for release details.

978-1-098-14224-7

[LSI]

For my wife, Navita, and our cherished son, Niall.

—Sameer

For my boys, whose smiles, hugs, and spirits make me a better person.

—Sébastien

For Mathilde, and for our wonderful children, Mélie and Anouk.

—Jonathan

Table of Contents

Preface

Welcome to *Kubernetes Cookbook*, and thanks for choosing it! With this book, we want to help you solve concrete problems around Kubernetes. We've compiled more than 100 recipes covering topics such as setting up a cluster, managing containerized workloads using Kubernetes API objects, using storage primitives, configuring security, and plenty more. Whether you are new to Kubernetes or have been using it for a while, we hope you'll find something useful here to improve your experience and use of Kubernetes.

Who Should Read This Book

This book was written for anyone who belongs somewhere in the DevOps spectrum. You might be an application developer who is required to occasionally interact with Kubernetes, or a platform engineer creating reusable solutions for other engineers in your organization, or anywhere in between. This book will help you navigate your way successfully through the Kubernetes jungle, from development to production. It covers core Kubernetes concepts as well as solutions from the broader ecosystem that have almost become de facto standards in the industry.

Why We Wrote This Book

Collectively, we have been part of the Kubernetes community for many years and have seen the many issues beginners and even more advanced users run into. We wanted to share the knowledge we've gathered running Kubernetes in production, as well as developing on and in Kubernetes—i.e., contributing to the core codebase or the ecosystem and writing applications that run on Kubernetes. It made perfect sense to work on the second edition of this book, considering that Kubernetes adoption has continued to grow in the years since the first edition of the book was published.

Navigating This Book

This cookbook contains 15 chapters. Each chapter is composed of recipes written in the standard O'Reilly recipe format (Problem, Solution, Discussion). You can read this book from front to back or skip to a specific chapter or recipe. Each recipe is independent of the others, and when an understanding of concepts from other recipes is needed, appropriate references are provided. The index is also an extremely powerful resource because sometimes a recipe is also showcasing a specific command, and the index highlights these connections.

A Note on Kubernetes Releases

At the time of writing, Kubernetes 1.27 (*https://oreil.ly/3b2Ta*) was the latest stable version, released at the end of April 2023, and this is the version we're using throughout the book as the baseline. However, the solutions presented here should, in general, work for older releases; we will call it out explicitly if this is not the case, mentioning the minimum required version.

Kubernetes follows a three-releases-per-year cadence. A release cycle has a length of approximately 15 weeks; for example, 1.26 was released in December 2022, 1.27 in April 2023, and 1.28 in August 2023, as this book was entering production. The Kubernetes release versioning guidelines (*https://oreil.ly/9eFLs*) indicate that you can expect support for a feature for the most recent three minor releases. Kubernetes Community supports active patch release series for a period of roughly 14 months. This means the stable API objects in the 1.27 release will be supported until at least June 2024. However, because the recipes in this book most often use only stable APIs, if you use a newer Kubernetes release, the recipes should still work.

Technology You Need to Understand

This intermediate-level book requires a minimal understanding of a few development and system administration concepts. Before diving into the book, you might want to review the following:

bash (Unix shell)
> This is the default Unix shell on Linux and macOS. Familiarity with the Unix shell, such as for editing files, setting file permissions and user privileges, moving files around the filesystem, and doing some basic shell programming, will be beneficial. For a general introduction, consult books such as Cameron Newham's *Learning the bash Shell*, Third Edition, or Carl Albing and JP Vossen's *bash Cookbook*, Second Edition, both from O'Reilly.

Package management

The tools in this book often have multiple dependencies that need to be met by installing some packages. Knowledge of the package management system on your machine is therefore required. It could be *apt* on Ubuntu/Debian systems, *yum* on CentOS/RHEL systems, or *Homebrew* on macOS. Whatever it is, make sure that you know how to install, upgrade, and remove packages.

Git

Git has established itself as the standard for distributed version control. If you are not already familiar with Git, we recommend *Version Control with Git*, Third Edition, by Prem Kumar Ponuthorai and Jon Loeliger (O'Reilly) as a good place to start. Together with Git, the GitHub website (*http://github.com*) is a great resource to get started with a hosted repository of your own. To learn about GitHub, check out the GitHub Training Kit site (*http://training.github.com*).

Go

Kubernetes is written in Go. Go has established itself as a popular programming language more broadly in the Kubernetes community and beyond. This cookbook is not about Go programming, but it shows how to compile a few Go projects. Some minimal understanding of how to set up a Go workspace will be handy. If you want to know more, a good place to start is the O'Reilly video training course *Introduction to Go Programming*.

Conventions Used in This Book

The following typographical conventions are used in this book:

Italic

Indicates new terms, URLs, email addresses, filenames, and file extensions.

`Constant width`

Used for program listings, as well as within paragraphs to refer to program elements such as variable or function names, databases, data types, environment variables, statements, and keywords. Also used for commands and command-line output.

`Constant width bold`

Shows commands or other text that should be typed literally by the user.

`Constant width italic`

Shows text that should be replaced with user-supplied values or by values determined by context.

This element signifies a tip or suggestion.

This element signifies a general note.

This element indicates a warning or caution.

Using Code Examples

Supplemental material (Kubernetes manifests, code examples, exercises, etc.) is available for download at *https://github.com/k8s-cookbook/recipes*. You can clone this repository, go to the relevant chapter and recipe, and use the code as is:

```
$ git clone https://github.com/k8s-cookbook/recipes
```

The examples in this repo are not meant to represent optimized setups to be used in production. They give you the basic minimum required to run the examples in the recipes.

If you have a technical question or a problem using the code examples, please send email to *support@oreilly.com*.

This book is here to help you get your job done. In general, if example code is offered with this book, you may use it in your programs and documentation. You do not need to contact us for permission unless you're reproducing a significant portion of the code. For example, writing a program that uses several chunks of code from this book does not require permission. Selling or distributing a CD-ROM of examples from O'Reilly books does require permission. Answering a question by citing this book and quoting example code does not require permission. Incorporating a significant amount of example code from this book into your product's documentation does require permission.

We appreciate, but do not require, attribution. An attribution usually includes the title, author, publisher, and ISBN. For example: "*Kubernetes Cookbook*, by Sameer Naik, Sébastien Goasguen, and Jonathan Michaux (O'Reilly). Copyright 2024 Cloud-Tank SARL, Sameer Naik, and Jonathan Michaux, 978-1-098-14224-7."

If you feel your use of code examples falls outside fair use or the permission given above, feel free to contact us at *permissions@oreilly.com*.

O'Reilly Online Learning

 For more than 40 years, *O'Reilly Media* has provided technology and business training, knowledge, and insight to help companies succeed.

Our unique network of experts and innovators share their knowledge and expertise through books, articles, and our online learning platform. O'Reilly's online learning platform gives you on-demand access to live training courses, in-depth learning paths, interactive coding environments, and a vast collection of text and video from O'Reilly and 200+ other publishers. For more information, visit *https://oreilly.com*.

How to Contact Us

Please address comments and questions concerning this book to the publisher:

O'Reilly Media, Inc.
1005 Gravenstein Highway North
Sebastopol, CA 95472
800-889-8969 (in the United States or Canada)
707-829-7019 (international or local)
707-829-0104 (fax)
support@oreilly.com
https://www.oreilly.com/about/contact.html

We have a web page for this book where we list errata, examples, and any additional information. You can access this page at *https://oreil.ly/kubernetes-cookbook-2e*.

For news and information about our books and courses, visit *https://oreilly.com*.

Find us on LinkedIn: *https://linkedin.com/company/oreilly-media*.

Follow us on Twitter: *https://twitter.com/oreillymedia*.

Watch us on YouTube: *https://youtube.com/oreillymedia*.

Acknowledgments

Thank you to the entire Kubernetes community for developing such amazing software and for being a great bunch of people—open, kind, and always ready to help.

Sameer and Jonathan were honored to work with Sébastien on the second edition of this book. We are all thankful for the reviews provided by Roland Huß, Jonathan Johnson, and Benjamin Muschko, who were invaluable in improving the finished product. We are also grateful to John Devins, Jeff Bleiel, and Ashley Stussy, our editors at O'Reilly, who were a pleasure to work with.

## CHAPTER 1

Getting Started with Kubernetes

In this first chapter we present recipes that will help you get started with Kubernetes. We show you how to use Kubernetes without installing it and introduce components such as the command-line interface (CLI) and the dashboard, which allow you to interact with a cluster, as well as Minikube, an all-in-one solution you can run on your laptop.

1.1 Installing the Kubernetes CLI, kubectl

Problem

You want to install the Kubernetes command-line interface so you can interact with your Kubernetes cluster.

Solution

The easiest option is to download the latest official release. For example, on a Linux system, to get the latest stable version, enter the following:

```
$ wget https://dl.k8s.io/release/$(wget -qO - https://dl.k8s.io/release/
stable.txt)/bin/linux/amd64/kubectl

$ sudo install -m 755 kubectl /usr/local/bin/kubectl
```

Using the Homebrew package manager (*https://brew.sh*), Linux and macOS users can also install kubectl:

```
$ brew install kubectl
```

After installation, make sure you have a working kubectl by listing its version:

```
$ kubectl version --client
Client Version: v1.28.0
Kustomize Version: v5.0.4-0.20230...
```

Discussion

kubectl is the official Kubernetes CLI and is available as open source software, which means you could build the kubectl binary yourself if you needed. See Recipe 15.1 to learn about compiling the Kubernetes source code locally.

It's useful to note that Google Kubernetes Engine users (see Recipe 2.11) can install kubectl using gcloud:

```
$ gcloud components install kubectl
```

Also note that in the latest versions of Minikube (see Recipe 1.2), you can invoke kubectl as a subcommand of minikube to run a kubectl binary that matches the cluster version:

```
$ minikube kubectl -- version --client
Client Version: version.Info{Major:"1", Minor:"27", GitVersion:"v1.27.4", ...}
Kustomize Version: v5.0.1
```

See Also

- Documentation on installing kubectl (*https://oreil.ly/DgK8a*)

1.2 Installing Minikube to Run a Local Kubernetes Instance

Problem

You want to use Kubernetes for testing or development or for training purposes on your local machine.

Solution

Minikube (*https://oreil.ly/97IFg*) is a tool that lets you easily use Kubernetes on your local machine.

To install the Minikube CLI locally, you can get the latest prebuilt release or build from source. To install the latest release of minikube on a Linux-based machine, do this:

```
$ wget https://storage.googleapis.com/minikube/releases/latest/
minikube-linux-amd64 -O minikube
```

```
$ sudo install -m 755 minikube /usr/local/bin/minikube
```

This will put the minikube binary in your path and make it accessible from everywhere.

Once it's installed, you can verify the Minikube version with the following command:

```
$ minikube version
minikube version: v1.31.2
commit: fd7ecd...
```

Discussion

Minikube can be deployed as a virtual machine, a container, or bare metal. This is configured using the --driver flag while creating a cluster on Minikube. When this flag is not specified, Minikube will automatically select the best available runtime environment.

A *hypervisor* is a software or hardware component that creates and manages virtual machines. It is responsible for allocating and managing the physical resources (CPU, memory, storage, network) of a host system and allowing multiple virtual machines (VMs) to run concurrently on the same physical hardware. Minikube supports a range of hypervisors, such as VirtualBox (*https://oreil.ly/-tbK7*), Hyperkit (*https://oreil.ly/djLvh*), Docker Desktop (*https://oreil.ly/xQ-mj*), Hyper-V (*https://oreil.ly/5EAe0*), and so on. The drivers (*https://oreil.ly/Y1jpt*) page gives an overview of the supported runtimes.

Minikube can also use a container runtime to create a cluster on a host machine. This driver is available only on a Linux-based host, where it's possible to run Linux containers natively without having to use a VM. While a container-based runtime does not offer the same level of isolation as a virtual machine, it does offer the best performance and resource utilization. At the time of writing, Minikube has support for Docker Engine (*https://oreil.ly/7gZPf*) and Podman (*https://oreil.ly/y6N3t*) (experimental).

Other tools that can be used for running local Kubernetes clusters using Linux containers are as follows:

- Kubernetes in Docker Desktop (see Recipe 1.6)
- kind (see Recipe 1.5)
- k3d (*https://k3d.io*)

See Also

- Minikube Get Started! guide (*https://oreil.ly/2b1fA*)
- Minikube drivers (*https://oreil.ly/HAZgT*)
- minikube source on GitHub (*https://oreil.ly/HmCEJ*)

1.3 Using Minikube Locally for Development

Problem

You want to use Minikube locally for testing and development of your Kubernetes application. You have installed and started minikube (see Recipe 1.2) and want to know a few extra commands to simplify your development experience.

Solution

Use the minikube start command to create a Kubernetes cluster locally:

```
$ minikube start
```

By default the cluster will be allocated 2 GB of RAM. If you don't like the defaults, you can override parameters such as the memory and number of CPUs, as well as picking a certain Kubernetes version for the Minikube VM—for example:

```
$ minikube start --cpus=4 --memory=4096 --kubernetes-version=v1.27.0
```

Additionally, you can specify the number of cluster nodes by overriding the default value of one node:

```
$ minikube start --cpus=2 --memory=4096 --nodes=2
```

To inspect the status of the Minikube cluster, do this:

```
$ minikube status
minikube
type: Control Plane
host: Running
kubelet: Running
apiserver: Running
kubeconfig: Configured

minikube-m02
type: Worker
host: Running
kubelet: Running
```

Similarly, to inspect the status of the Kubernetes cluster running inside Minikube, do this:

```
$ kubectl cluster-info
Kubernetes control plane is running at https://192.168.64.72:8443
CoreDNS is running at https://192.168.64.72:8443/api/v1/namespaces/
kube-system/services/kube-dns:dns/proxy

To further debug and diagnose cluster problems, use 'kubectl cluster-info dump'.
```

The Kubernetes cluster created with Minikube utilizes resources of the host machine, so you need to make sure your host has the resources available. More importantly, when you are done, do not forget to stop it with minikube stop to release the system resources.

Discussion

The Minikube CLI offers commands that make your life easier. The CLI has built-in help that you can use to discover the subcommands on your own—here's a snippet:

```
$ minikube
...
Basic Commands:
  start           Starts a local Kubernetes cluster
  status          Gets the status of a local Kubernetes cluster
  stop            Stops a running local Kubernetes cluster
  delete          Deletes a local Kubernetes cluster
...
Configuration and Management Commands:
  addons          Enable or disable a minikube addon
...
```

Aside from start, stop, and delete, you should become familiar with the ip, ssh, tunnel, dashboard, and docker-env commands.

If for any reason your Minikube becomes unstable or you want to start fresh, you can remove it with minikube stop and minikube delete. Then minikube start will give you a fresh installation.

1.4 Starting Your First Application on Minikube

Problem

You've started Minikube (see Recipe 1.3), and now you want to launch your first application on Kubernetes.

Solution

As an example, you can start the Ghost (*https://ghost.org*) microblogging platform on Minikube using two kubectl commands:

```
$ kubectl run ghost --image=ghost:5.59.4 --env="NODE_ENV=development"
$ kubectl expose pod ghost --port=2368 --type=NodePort
```

Monitor the pod manually to see when it starts running:

```
$ kubectl get pods
NAME                      READY    STATUS    RESTARTS    AGE
ghost-8449997474-kn86m    1/1      Running   0           24s
```

Now you can use the minikube service command to automatically load the application service URL in the web browser:

```
$ minikube service ghost
```

Discussion

The kubectl run command is called a *generator*; it is a convenience command to create a Pod object (see Recipe 4.4). The kubectl expose command is also a generator, a convenience command to create a Service object (see Recipe 5.1) that routes network traffic to the containers started by your deployment.

When you do not need the application anymore, you can remove the Pod to release the cluster resources:

```
$ kubectl delete pod ghost
```

Additionally, you should delete the ghost service that was created by the kubectl expose command:

```
$ kubectl delete svc ghost
```

1.5 Using kind to Run Kubernetes Locally

Problem

kind (*https://kind.sigs.k8s.io*) is an alternative way to run Kubernetes locally. It was originally designed for testing Kubernetes but is now also often used as a way to try Kubernetes-native solutions on a laptop with minimal fuss. You want to use kind locally for testing and developing your Kubernetes application.

Solution

The minimum requirements for using kind are Go and a Docker runtime. kind is easy to install (*https://oreil.ly/1MxZo*) on any platform, for example using `brew`:

```
$ brew install kind
```

Then, creating a cluster is as simple as doing this:

```
$ kind create cluster
```

Deleting it is just as easy:

```
$ kind delete cluster
```

Discussion

Because kind was originally developed for testing Kubernetes, one of its core design principles (*https://oreil.ly/jNTNx*) is that it should lend itself well to automation. You might want to consider using kind if you plan on automatically deploying Kubernetes clusters for testing purposes.

See Also

- The official kind Quick Start guide (*https://oreil.ly/aXjcY*)

1.6 Using Kubernetes in Docker Desktop

Problem

Docker Desktop is an offering built on top of Docker Engine that provides a number of useful developer tools, including a built-in version of Kubernetes and an associated load balancer to route traffic into the cluster. This means you can install a single tool and have access to pretty much everything you need to get started locally. You want to use Docker Desktop locally for testing and developing your Kubernetes application.

Solution

Install Docker Desktop (*https://oreil.ly/HKVaR*) and make sure to enable Kubernetes during the installation process.

You can activate and deactivate Kubernetes from Docker Desktop's settings panel, as shown in Figure 1-1. You might want to do this if you're using Docker Desktop for its Docker Engine but aren't using Kubernetes, as this will save resources on your computer. As shown here, the settings panel also shows you which version of Kubernetes is provided by Docker Desktop, which can be useful when debugging as certain solutions might have requirements on the minimum or maximum version of Kubernetes that they can run on.

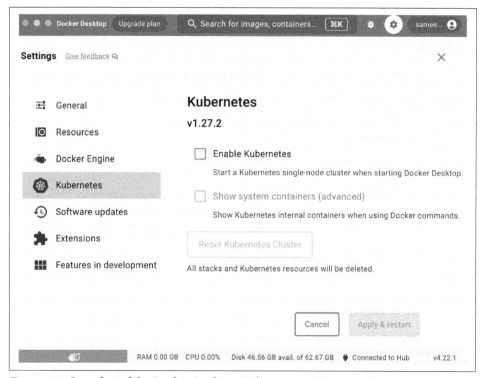

Figure 1-1. Snapshot of the Docker Desktop Kubernetes settings panel

It is worth noting that the version of Kubernetes embedded into Docker Desktop lags behind the latest Kubernetes release by a few versions, whereas Minikube tends to be more up to date.

As shown in Figure 1-2, the Docker Desktop toolbar menu lets you easily switch kubectl contexts between different local clusters, which means you can have Minikube and Docker Desktop's Kubernetes running at the same time but switch between them (not that we recommend doing this). For information on how to do this directly from kubectl, see Recipe 1.7.

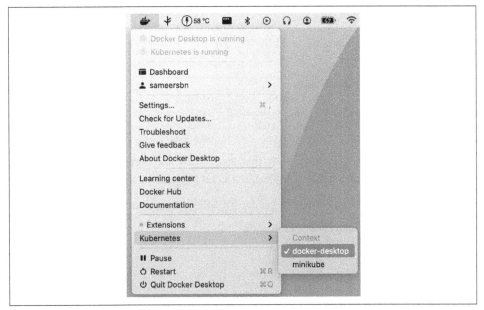

Figure 1-2. Snapshot of the Docker Desktop context switcher for `kubectl`

Discussion

Although it is a quick and easy way to get started with Kubernetes, be aware that Docker Desktop is not open source, and that the free version is restricted for use by individuals, small businesses, students and educators, and non-commercial open source developers.

Docker Engine, on the other hand, which can be used to run Minikube, has an Apache 2.0 license, as does Minikube itself.

1.7 Switching kubectl Contexts

Problem

`kubectl` is always configured to speak to a given Kubernetes cluster by default, and this configuration is part of something called the *context*. If you've forgotten which cluster `kubectl` is set to, want to switch between clusters, or want to change other context-related parameters, then this recipe is for you.

Solution

To view the contexts available to kubectl, use the kubectl config get-contexts command:

```
$ kubectl config get-contexts
CURRENT   NAME            CLUSTER         AUTHINFO        NAMESPACE
          docker-desktop  docker-desktop  docker-desktop
          kind-kind       kind-kind       kind-kind
*         minikube        minikube        minikube        default
```

As you can see from the output, in this case there are three Kubernetes clusters available to kubectl, and the current context is set to speak to the minikube cluster.

To switch to the kind-kind cluster, execute the following command:

```
$ kubectl config use-context kind-kind
Switched to context "kind-kind".
```

Discussion

If you want to use your local kubectl to access a remote cluster, you can do so by editing the kubeconfig file. Learn more about the kubeconfig file in the official documentation (*https://oreil.ly/jMZ3h*).

1.8 Switching Contexts and Namespaces Using kubectx and kubens

Problem

You want to find an easier way to switch contexts (i.e., clusters) and namespaces with kubectl, as the commands for switching contexts are long and quite hard to remember.

Solution

kubectx and kubens are a couple of popular open source scripts that make it much easier to switch contexts for kubectl and to switch namespaces so that you don't have to explicitly set the namespace name for every command.

There are plenty of available installation options. If you're able to use brew, then you can try this:

```
$ brew install kubectx
```

You can then easily list the available kubectl contexts like so:

```
$ kubectx
docker-desktop
kind-kind
minikube
```

and switch contexts just as easily:

```
$ kubectx minikube
Switched to context "minikube".
```

Similarly, kubens lets you easily list and switch namespaces:

```
$ kubens
default
kube-node-lease
kube-public
kube-system
test
```

```
$ kubens test
default
Context "minikube" modified.
Active namespace is "test".
```

All commands from then onward will be performed in the context of the chosen namespace:

```
$ kubectl get pods
default
No resources found in test namespace.
```

See Also

- The repository for the kubectl and kubens tools (*https://oreil.ly/QBH3N*)

## CHAPTER 2

Creating a Kubernetes Cluster

In this chapter we discuss multiple ways to set up a full-blown Kubernetes cluster. We cover low-level, standardized tooling (kubeadm) that also serves as the basis for other installers and show you where to find the relevant binaries for the control plane, as well as for worker nodes. We demonstrate how to write systemd unit files to supervise Kubernetes components and finally show how to set up clusters on Google Cloud Platform and Azure.

2.1 Preparing a New Node for a Kubernetes Cluster

Problem

You want to prepare a new node with all the required tooling to create a new Kubernetes cluster or add to an existing cluster.

Solution

To prepare an Ubuntu-based host for a Kubernetes cluster, you first need to turn on IPv4 forwarding and enable iptables to see bridged traffic:

```
$ cat <<EOF | sudo tee /etc/modules-load.d/k8s.conf
overlay
br_netfilter
EOF

$ sudo modprobe overlay
$ sudo modprobe br_netfilter

$ cat <<EOF | sudo tee /etc/sysctl.d/k8s.conf
net.bridge.bridge-nf-call-iptables  = 1
net.bridge.bridge-nf-call-ip6tables = 1
```

```
net.ipv4.ip_forward = 1
EOF

$ sudo sysctl --system
```

For compatibility with the kubeadm tool, the swap needs to be turned off on the node:

```
$ sudo apt install cron -y
$ sudo swapoff -a
$ (sudo crontab -l 2>/dev/null; echo "@reboot /sbin/swapoff -a") | sudo crontab -
|| true
```

Cluster nodes require an implementation of the Kubernetes Container Runtime Interface (CRI). cri-o (*https://cri-o.io*) is one such implementation. The cri-o version should match the Kubernetes version. For example, if you are bootstrapping a Kubernetes 1.27 cluster, configure the VERSION variable accordingly:

```
$ VERSION="1.27"
$ OS="xUbuntu_22.04"

$ cat <<EOF | sudo tee /etc/apt/sources.list.d/devel:kubic:libcontainers:
stable.list
deb https://download.opensuse.org/repositories/devel:/kubic:/libcontainers:
/stable/$OS/ /
EOF

$ cat <<EOF | sudo tee /etc/apt/sources.list.d/devel:kubic:libcontainers:
stable:cri-o:$VERSION.list
deb http://download.opensuse.org/repositories/devel:/kubic:/libcontainers:
/stable:/cri-o:/$VERSION/$OS/ /
EOF

$ curl -L https://download.opensuse.org/repositories/devel:/kubic:/libcontainers:
/stable:/cri-o:/$VERSION/$OS/Release.key | \
    sudo apt-key add -
$ curl -L https://download.opensuse.org/repositories/devel:/kubic:/libcontainers:
/stable/$OS/Release.key | \
    sudo apt-key add -

$ sudo apt-get update

$ sudo apt-get install cri-o cri-o-runc cri-tools -y
```

Then reload the systemd configurations and enable cri-o:

```
$ sudo systemctl daemon-reload
$ sudo systemctl enable crio --now
```

The kubeadm tool is required to bootstrap a Kubernetes cluster from scratch as well as to join an existing cluster. Enable its software repository with this:

```
$ cat <<EOF | sudo tee /etc/apt/sources.list.d/kubernetes.list
deb [signed-by=/etc/apt/keyrings/k8s-archive-keyring.gpg]
https://apt.kubernetes.io/
```

```
kubernetes-xenial main
EOF

$ sudo apt-get install -y apt-transport-https ca-certificates curl
$ sudo curl -fsSLo /etc/apt/keyrings/k8s-archive-keyring.gpg \
    https://dl.k8s.io/apt/doc/apt-key.gpg

$ sudo apt-get update
```

Now you can install all the tools required to bootstrap a Kubernetes cluster node. You will need the following:

- The kubelet binary
- The kubeadm CLI
- The kubectl client

Run this command to install them:

```
$ sudo apt-get install -y kubelet kubeadm kubectl
```

Then mark these packages as held back, which will prevent them from being automatically upgraded:

```
$ sudo apt-mark hold kubelet kubeadm kubectl
```

Your Ubuntu host is now ready to be part of a Kubernetes cluster.

Discussion

kubeadm is a setup tool that provides kubeadm init and kubeadm join. kubeadm init is used to bootstrap a Kubernetes control-plane node, while kubeadm join is used to bootstrap a worker node and join it to the cluster. In essence, kubeadm provides the actions necessary to get a minimum viable cluster up and running. kubelet is the *node agent* that runs on each node.

In addition to cri-o, other container runtimes worth investigating are containerd (*https://oreil.ly/M1kDx*), Docker Engine (*https://oreil.ly/P5_l_*), and Mirantis Container Runtime (*https://oreil.ly/BEWaG*).

2.2 Bootstrapping a Kubernetes Control-Plane Node

Problem

You have initialized an Ubuntu host for Kubernetes (see Recipe 2.1) and now need to bootstrap a new Kubernetes control-plane node.

Solution

With the kubeadm binary installed, you are ready to start bootstrapping your Kubernetes cluster. Initialize the control plane on the node with the following:

```
$ NODENAME=$(hostname -s)
$ IPADDR=$(ip route get 8.8.8.8 | sed -n 's/.*src \(([^\ ]*\).*/\1/p')
$ POD_CIDR=192.168.0.0/16
```

 The control-plane node should have a minimum of two vCPUs and 2 GB RAM.

Now initialize the control-plane node using kubeadm:

```
$ sudo kubeadm init --apiserver-advertise-address=$IPADDR \
    --apiserver-cert-extra-sans=$IPADDR  \
    --pod-network-cidr=$POD_CIDR \
    --node-name $NODENAME \
    --ignore-preflight-errors Swap
[init] Using Kubernetes version: v1.27.2
[preflight] Running pre-flight checks
[preflight] Pulling images required for setting up a Kubernetes cluster
...
```

The output of the init command contains the configuration for setting up kubectl to talk to your cluster. Once kubectl has been configured, you can verify the cluster component health status using the following command:

```
$ kubectl get --raw='/readyz?verbose'
```

To get the cluster information, use:

```
$ kubectl cluster-info
```

Discussion

User workloads are not scheduled to execute on the control-plane node. If you are creating an experimental single-node cluster, then you would need to taint the control-plane node to schedule user workloads on the control-plane node:

```
$ kubectl taint nodes --all node-role.kubernetes.io/control-plane-
```

See Also

- Creating a cluster with kubeadm (*https://oreil.ly/q9nwI*)

2.3 Installing a Container Network Add-on for Cluster Networking

Problem

You have bootstrapped a Kubernetes control-plane node (see Recipe 2.2) and now need to install a pod network add-on so that pods can communicate with each other.

Solution

You can install the Calico network add-on with the following command on the control-plane node:

```
$ kubectl apply -f https://raw.githubusercontent.com/projectcalico/calico/
v3.26.1/manifests/calico.yaml
```

Discussion

You must use a Container Network Interface (CNI) add-on that is compatible with your cluster and that suits your needs. There are a number of add-ons that implement the CNI. Take a look at the nonexhaustive list of available add-ons in the Kubernetes documentation (*https://oreil.ly/HosU6*).

2.4 Adding Worker Nodes to a Kubernetes Cluster

Problem

You have initialized your Kubernetes control-plane node (see Recipe 2.2) and installed a CNI add-on (see Recipe 2.3), and now you want to add worker nodes to your cluster.

Solution

With the Ubuntu host initialized for Kubernetes, as shown in Recipe 2.1, execute the following command on the control-plane node to display the cluster `join` command:

```
$ kubeadm token create --print-join-command
```

Now, execute the `join` command on the worker node:

```
$ sudo kubeadm join --token <token>
```

> The worker node should have a minimum of one vCPU and 2 GB RAM.

Head back to your control-plane node terminal session and you will see your nodes join:

```
$ kubectl get nodes
NAME     STATUS   ROLES           AGE   VERSION
master   Ready    control-plane   28m   v1.27.2
worker   Ready    <none>          10s   v1.27.2
```

You can repeat these steps to add more worker nodes to the Kubernetes cluster.

Discussion

Worker nodes are where your workloads run. When your cluster starts running out of resources, you will begin noticing the *Pending* status of new pods. At this point you should consider adding more resources to the cluster by adding more worker nodes.

2.5 Deploying the Kubernetes Dashboard

Problem

You have created a Kubernetes cluster, and now you want to create, view, and manage containerized workloads on the cluster using a user interface.

Solution

Use the Kubernetes dashboard (*https://oreil.ly/n7WQw*), which is a web-based user interface to deploy containerized applications to a Kubernetes cluster and to manage the cluster resources.

> If you're using Minikube, you can install the Kubernetes dashboard simply by enabling the dashboard add-on:
>
> ```
> $ minikube addons enable dashboard
> ```

To deploy the v2.7.0 Kubernetes dashboard, do this:

```
$ kubectl apply -f https://raw.githubusercontent.com/kubernetes/dashboard/
v2.7.0/aio/deploy/recommended.yaml
```

Then verify that the deployment is ready:

```
$ kubectl get deployment kubernetes-dashboard -n kubernetes-dashboard
NAME                   READY   UP-TO-DATE   AVAILABLE   AGE
kubernetes-dashboard   1/1     1            1           44s
```

2.6 Accessing the Kubernetes Dashboard

Problem

You have installed the Kubernetes dashboard (see Recipe 2.5) on your cluster, and you want to access the dashboard from a web browser.

Solution

You need to create a `ServiceAccount` (*https://oreil.ly/pXErB*) with privileges to administer the cluster. Create a file named *sa.yaml* with the following contents:

```
apiVersion: v1
kind: ServiceAccount
metadata:
  name: admin-user
  namespace: kubernetes-dashboard
---
apiVersion: rbac.authorization.k8s.io/v1
kind: ClusterRoleBinding
metadata:
  name: admin-user
roleRef:
  apiGroup: rbac.authorization.k8s.io
  kind: ClusterRole
  name: cluster-admin
subjects:
- kind: ServiceAccount
  name: admin-user
  namespace: kubernetes-dashboard
```

Create the `ServiceAccount` with this:

```
$ kubectl apply -f sa.yaml
```

To access the Kubernetes dashboard, you need to create an authentication token associated with this account. Save the token printed in the output of the following command:

```
$ kubectl -n kubernetes-dashboard create token admin-user
eyJhbGciOiJSUzI1NiIsImtpZCI6...
```

Since the Kubernetes dashboard is a cluster-local service, you need to set up a proxy connection to the cluster:

```
$ kubectl proxy
```

By visiting the site *http://localhost:8001/api/v1/namespaces/kubernetes-dashboard/serv ices/https:kubernetes-dashboard:/proxy/#/workloads?namespace=_all* you are now able to open the Kubernetes dashboard and authenticate yourself using the authentication token created earlier.

In the UI that opens in your browser, you will see the page depicted in Figure 2-1.

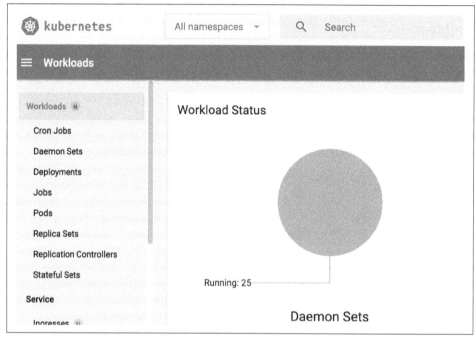

Figure 2-1. Snapshot of the dashboard application create view

 If you are using Minikube, all you need to do is:

```
$ minikube dashboard
```

Discussion

To create an application, click the plus sign (+) at the top-right corner, select the "Create from form" tab, give the application a name, and specify the container image you want to use. Then click the Deploy button and you will be presented with a new view that shows deployments, pods, and replica sets. In Kubernetes there are dozens of important resource types, such as deployments, pods, replica sets, services, and so on, that we will explore in greater detail in the rest of the book.

The snapshot in Figure 2-2 presents a typical dashboard view after having created a single application using the Redis container.

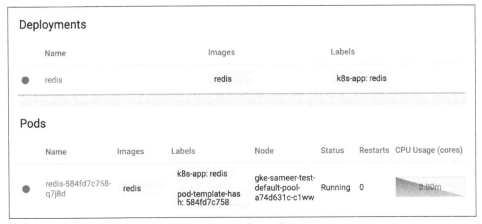

Figure 2-2. A dashboard overview with a Redis application

If you go back to a terminal session and use the command-line client, you will see the same thing:

```
$ kubectl get all
NAME                        READY   STATUS    RESTARTS   AGE
pod/redis-584fd7c758-vwl52   1/1     Running   0          5m9s

NAME                 TYPE        CLUSTER-IP   EXTERNAL-IP   PORT(S)   AGE
service/kubernetes   ClusterIP   10.96.0.1    <none>        443/TCP   19m

NAME                    READY   UP-TO-DATE   AVAILABLE   AGE
deployment.apps/redis   1/1     1            1           5m9s

NAME                              DESIRED   CURRENT   READY   AGE
replicaset.apps/redis-584fd7c758   1         1         1       5m9s
```

Your Redis pod will be running the Redis server, as the following logs show:

```
$ kubectl logs redis-3215927958-4x88v
...
1:C 25 Aug 2023 06:17:23.934 * oO0OoO0OoO0Oo Redis is starting oO0OoO0OoO0Oo
1:C 25 Aug 2023 06:17:23.934 * Redis version=7.2.0, bits=64, commit=00000000,
modified=0, pid=1, just started
1:C 25 Aug 2023 06:17:23.934 # Warning: no config file specified, using the
default config. In order to specify a config file use redis-server
/path/to/redis.conf
1:M 25 Aug 2023 06:17:23.934 * monotonic clock: POSIX clock_gettime
1:M 25 Aug 2023 06:17:23.934 * Running mode=standalone, port=6379.
1:M 25 Aug 2023 06:17:23.935 * Server initialized
1:M 25 Aug 2023 06:17:23.935 * Ready to accept connections tcp
```

2.7 Deploying the Kubernetes Metrics Server

Problem

You have deployed the Kubernetes dashboard (see Recipe 2.5) but don't see the CPU and memory usage information in the dashboard.

Solution

The Kubernetes dashboard requires the Kubernetes Metrics Server (*https://oreil.ly/BEHwR*) to visualize the CPU and memory usage.

 If you are using Minikube, you can install the Kubernetes Metrics Server simply by enabling the metrics-server add-on:

```
$ minikube addons enable metrics-server
```

To deploy the latest release of the Kubernetes Metrics Server, do this:

```
$ kubectl apply -f https://github.com/kubernetes-sigs/metrics-server/releases/
latest/download/components.yaml
```

Then verify that the deployment is ready:

```
$ kubectl get deployment metrics-server -n kube-system
NAME             READY   UP-TO-DATE   AVAILABLE   AGE
metrics-server   1/1     1            1           7m27s
```

If you see that the deployment is not entering the ready state, check the pod logs:

```
$ kubectl logs -f deployment/metrics-server -n kube-system
I0707 05:06:19.537981     1 server.go:187] "Failed probe"
probe="metric-storage-ready" err="no metrics to serve"
E0707 05:06:26.395852     1 scraper.go:140] "Failed to scrape node" err="Get
\"https://192.168.64.50:10250/metrics/resource\": x509: cannot validate
certificate for 192.168.64.50 because it doesn't contain any IP SANs"
node="minikube"
```

If you see the error message "cannot validate certificate," you need to append the flag --kubelet-insecure-tls to the Metrics Server deployment:

```
$ kubectl patch deployment metrics-server -n kube-system --type='json'
-p='[{"op": "add", "path": "/spec/template/spec/containers/0/args/-", "value":
"--kubelet-insecure-tls"}]'
```

It can take several minutes for the Metrics Server to become available after having started it. If it is not yet in the ready state, then requests for metrics might produce errors.

Once the Metrics Server has started, the Kubernetes dashboard will display the CPU and memory usage statistics, as shown in Figure 2-3.

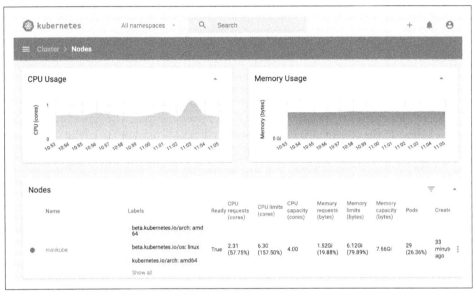

Figure 2-3. Dashboard cluster nodes view

Discussion

The node and pod metrics can also be viewed in the command line using the `kubectl top` command:

```
$ kubectl top pods -A
NAMESPACE      NAME                                    CPU(cores)    MEMORY(bytes)
kube-system    coredns-5d78c9869d-5fh78                9m            9Mi
kube-system    etcd-minikube                           164m          36Mi
kube-system    kube-apiserver-minikube                 322m          254Mi
kube-system    kube-controller-manager-minikube        123m          35Mi
kube-system    kube-proxy-rvl8v                         13m           12Mi
kube-system    kube-scheduler-minikube                 62m           15Mi
kube-system    storage-provisioner                     22m           7Mi
```

Similarly, to view the node metrics, do this:

```
$ kubectl top nodes
NAME        CPU(cores)    CPU%    MEMORY(bytes)    MEMORY%
minikube    415m          10%     1457Mi           18%
```

See Also

- Kubernetes Metrics Server GitHub repository (*https://oreil.ly/C_O6W*)
- Resource metrics pipeline documentation (*https://oreil.ly/ODZCr*)

2.8 Downloading a Kubernetes Release from GitHub

Problem

You want to download an official Kubernetes release instead of compiling from source.

Solution

The Kubernetes project publishes an archive for every release. The link to the archive can be found in the CHANGELOG file of the particular release. Go to the *CHANGE-LOG* folder of the project page (*https://oreil.ly/MMwRs*) and open the CHANGELOG file for the release of your choice. Within the file you will find a link to download the *kubernetes.tar.gz* file of that release.

For example, if you want to download the v1.28.0 release, go ahead and open *CHANGELOG-1.28.md*, and in the section titled "Downloads for v1.28.0" you will find the link to *kubernetes.tar.gz* (*https://dl.k8s.io/v1.28.0/kubernetes.tar.gz*).

```
$ wget https://dl.k8s.io/v1.28.0/kubernetes.tar.gz
```

If you want to compile Kubernetes from source, see Recipe 15.1.

Discussion

The CHANGELOG file also lists the sha512 hash of the *kubernetes.tar.gz* archive. It is recommended that you verify the integrity of the *kubernetes.tar.gz* archive to ensure that it has not been tampered with in any way. To do this, generate the sha512 hash of the downloaded archive locally and compare it with that of the one listed in the CHANGELOG:

```
$ sha512sum kubernetes.tar.gz
9aaf7cc004d09297dc7bbc1f0149....  kubernetes.tar.gz
```

2.9 Downloading Client and Server Binaries

Problem

You have downloaded a release archive (see Recipe 2.8), but it does not contain the actual binaries.

Solution

The release archive does not contain the release binaries (for the purpose of keeping the release archive small). Thus, you need to download the binaries separately. To do so, run the *get-kube-binaries.sh* script, as shown here:

```
$ tar -xvf kubernetes.tar.gz
$ cd kubernetes/cluster
$ ./get-kube-binaries.sh
```

Once complete, you will have the client binaries in *client/bin*:

```
$ ls ../client/bin
kubectl          kubectl-convert
```

and an archive containing the server binaries in *server/kubernetes*:

```
$ ls ../server/kubernetes
kubernetes-server-linux-amd64.tar.gz    kubernetes-manifests.tar.gz       README
...
```

Discussion

If you want to skip downloading the entire release archive and quickly download the client and server binaries, you can get them directly from Download Kubernetes (*https://oreil.ly/tdN0P*). On this page you will find direct links to binaries for various operating system and architecture combinations, as shown in Figure 2-4.

OPERATING SYSTEMS				ARCHITECTUR			
darwin	linux	windows		386	amd64	arm	arm64

Version	Operating System	Architecture	Download Binary	Copy Lir
v1.28.3	darwin	amd64	kubectl	▊ dl.k8
v1.28.3	darwin	amd64	kubectl-convert	▊ dl.k8
v1.28.3	darwin	arm64	kubectl	▊ dl.k8
v1.28.3	darwin	arm64	kubectl-convert	▊ dl.k8

Figure 2-4. downloadkubernetes.com, listing binaries of the Kubernetes v1.28.0 release for the Darwin operating system

2.10 Using systemd Unit Files for Running Kubernetes Components

Problem

You have used Minikube (see Recipe 1.2) for learning and know how to bootstrap a Kubernetes cluster using kubeadm (see Recipe 2.2), but you want to install a cluster from scratch.

Solution

To do so, you need to run the Kubernetes components using systemd unit files. You are looking only for basic examples to run the kubelet via systemd.

Inspecting how kubeadm configures the Kubernetes daemons to launch using systemd unit files helps you understand how to do it on your own. If you look closely at the kubeadm configuration, you will see that the kubelet is running on every node in your cluster, including the control-plane node.

Here is an example, which you can reproduce by logging in to any node of a cluster built with kubeadm (see Recipe 2.2):

```
$ systemctl status kubelet
● kubelet.service - kubelet: The Kubernetes Node Agent
    Loaded: loaded (/lib/systemd/system/kubelet.service; enabled;
    vendor preset: enabled)
   Drop-In: /etc/systemd/system/kubelet.service.d
            └─10-kubeadm.conf
    Active: active (running) since Tue 2023-05-30 04:21:29 UTC; 2h 49min ago
      Docs: https://kubernetes.io/docs/home/
  Main PID: 797 (kubelet)
     Tasks: 11 (limit: 2234)
    Memory: 40.2M
       CPU: 5min 14.792s
    CGroup: /system.slice/kubelet.service
            └─797 /usr/bin/kubelet \
                --bootstrap-kubeconfig=/etc/kubernetes/bootstrap-kubelet.conf \
                --kubeconfig=/etc/kubernetes/kubelet.conf \
                --config=/var/lib/kubelet/config.yaml \
                --container-runtime-endpoint=unix:///var/run/crio/crio.sock \
                --pod-infra-container-image=registry.k8s.io/pause:3.9
```

This gives you a link to the systemd unit file in */lib/systemd/system/kubelet.service* and its configuration in */etc/systemd/system/kubelet.service.d/10-kubeadm.conf*.

The unit file is straightforward—it points to the kubelet binary installed in */usr/bin*:

```
[Unit]
Description=kubelet: The Kubernetes Node Agent
```

```
Documentation=https://kubernetes.io/docs/home/
Wants=network-online.target
After=network-online.target

[Service]
ExecStart=/usr/bin/kubelet
Restart=always
StartLimitInterval=0
RestartSec=10

[Install]
WantedBy=multi-user.target
```

The configuration file tells you how the kubelet binary is started:

```
[Service]
Environment="KUBELET_KUBECONFIG_ARGS=--bootstrap-kubeconfig=/etc/kubernetes/
bootstrap-kubelet.conf --kubeconfig=/etc/kubernetes/kubelet.conf"
Environment="KUBELET_CONFIG_ARGS=--config=/var/lib/kubelet/config.yaml"
EnvironmentFile=-/var/lib/kubelet/kubeadm-flags.env
EnvironmentFile=-/etc/default/kubelet

ExecStart=
ExecStart=/usr/bin/kubelet $KUBELET_KUBECONFIG_ARGS $KUBELET_CONFIG_ARGS
$KUBELET_KUBEADM_ARGS $KUBELET_EXTRA_ARGS
```

All the options specified, such as --kubeconfig, defined by the environment variable $KUBELET_CONFIG_ARGS, are start-up options (*https://oreil.ly/quccc*) of the kubelet binary.

Discussion

systemd (*https://oreil.ly/RmuZp*) is a system and services manager, sometimes referred to as an *init system*. It is now the default services manager on Ubuntu and CentOS.

The unit file just shown deals only with the kubelet. You can write your own unit files for all the other components of a Kubernetes cluster (i.e., API server, controller manager, scheduler, proxy). Kubernetes the Hard Way (*https://oreil.ly/AWnxD*) has examples of unit files for each component.

However, you only need to run the kubelet. Indeed, note that the configuration option --pod-manifest-path allows you to pass a directory where the kubelet will look for manifests that it will automatically start. With kubeadm, this directory is used to pass the manifests of the API server, scheduler, etcd, and controller manager. Hence, Kubernetes manages itself, and the only thing managed by systemd is the kubelet process.

To illustrate this, you can list the contents of the */etc/kubernetes/manifests* directory in your kubeadm-based cluster:

```
$ ls -l /etc/kubernetes/manifests
total 16
-rw------- 1 root root 2393 May 29 11:04 etcd.yaml
-rw------- 1 root root 3882 May 29 11:04 kube-apiserver.yaml
-rw------- 1 root root 3394 May 29 11:04 kube-controller-manager.yaml
-rw------- 1 root root 1463 May 29 11:04 kube-scheduler.yaml
```

Looking at the details of the *etcd.yaml* manifest, you can see that it is a Pod with a single container that runs etcd:

```
$ cat /etc/kubernetes/manifests/etcd.yaml

apiVersion: v1
kind: Pod
metadata:
  annotations:
    kubeadm.kubernetes.io/etcd.advertise-client-urls: https://10.10.100.30:2379
  creationTimestamp: null
  labels:
    component: etcd
    tier: control-plane
  name: etcd
  namespace: kube-system
spec:
  containers:
  - command:
    - etcd
    - --advertise-client-urls=https://10.10.100.30:2379
    - --cert-file=/etc/kubernetes/pki/etcd/server.crt
    - --client-cert-auth=true
    - --data-dir=/var/lib/etcd
    - --experimental-initial-corrupt-check=true
    - --experimental-watch-progress-notify-interval=5s
    - --initial-advertise-peer-urls=https://10.10.100.30:2380
    - --initial-cluster=master=https://10.10.100.30:2380
    - --key-file=/etc/kubernetes/pki/etcd/server.key
    - --listen-client-urls=https://127.0.0.1:2379,https://10.10.100.30:2379
    - --listen-metrics-urls=http://127.0.0.1:2381
    - --listen-peer-urls=https://10.10.100.30:2380
    - --name=master
    - --peer-cert-file=/etc/kubernetes/pki/etcd/peer.crt
    - --peer-client-cert-auth=true
    - --peer-key-file=/etc/kubernetes/pki/etcd/peer.key
    - --peer-trusted-ca-file=/etc/kubernetes/pki/etcd/ca.crt
    - --snapshot-count=10000
    - --trusted-ca-file=/etc/kubernetes/pki/etcd/ca.crt
    image: registry.k8s.io/etcd:3.5.7-0
    ...
```

See Also

- kubelet configuration options (*https://oreil.ly/E95yp*)

2.11 Creating a Kubernetes Cluster on Google Kubernetes Engine

Problem

You want to create a Kubernetes cluster on Google Kubernetes Engine (GKE).

Solution

To use GKE, you first need a few things:

- A Google Cloud Platform (GCP) (*https://oreil.ly/CAiDf*) account with billing enabled
- A GCP project with GKE (*https://oreil.ly/eGX2n*) enabled
- Google Cloud SDK (*https://oreil.ly/Y00rC*) installed

The Google Cloud SDK contains the `gcloud` CLI tool for interacting with GCP services from the command line. After the SDK has been installed, authenticate `gcloud` to access your GCP project:

```
$ gcloud auth login
```

Using the `gcloud` command-line interface, create a Kubernetes cluster with the `container clusters create` command, like so:

```
$ gcloud container clusters create oreilly --zone us-east1-b
```

By default this will create a Kubernetes cluster with three worker nodes in the zone or region specified. The master node is being managed by the GKE service and cannot be accessed.

 If you're unsure what zone or region (*https://oreil.ly/4Bvua*) to use for the `--zone` or `--region` argument, execute `gcloud compute zones list` or `gcloud compute regions list` and pick one near you. Zones are typically less resource hungry than regions.

Once you are done using your cluster, do not forget to delete it to avoid being charged:

```
$ gcloud container clusters delete oreilly --zone us-east1-b
```

Discussion

You can skip the `gcloud` CLI installation by using the Google Cloud Shell (*https://oreil.ly/E-Qcr*), a pure online browser-based solution.

You can list your existing GKE clusters using this command:

```
$ gcloud container clusters list --zone us-east1-b
NAME     ZONE       MASTER_VERSION   MASTER_IP      ...  STATUS
oreilly  us-east1-b 1.24.9-gke.2000  35.187.80.94   ...  RUNNING
```

 The gcloud CLI allows you to resize your cluster, update it, and upgrade it:

```
...
COMMANDS
...
    resize
        Resizes an existing cluster for running
        containers.
    update
        Update cluster settings for an existing container
        cluster.
    upgrade
        Upgrade the Kubernetes version of an existing
        container cluster.
```

See Also

- GKE quickstart (*https://oreil.ly/WMDSx*)
- Google Cloud Shell quickstart (*https://oreil.ly/_w0va*)

2.12 Creating a Kubernetes Cluster on Azure Kubernetes Service

Problem

You want to create a Kubernetes cluster on Azure Kubernetes Service (AKS).

Solution

To create an AKS cluster, you will need the following:

- A Microsoft Azure portal account (*https://oreil.ly/PyUA0*)
- Azure CLI (*https://oreil.ly/An7xM*) installed

First, make sure that you have Azure CLI version 2.0 or higher installed and then log in to Azure:

```
$ az --version | grep "^azure-cli"
azure-cli                      2.50.0 *

$ az login
To sign in, use a web browser to open the page https://aka.ms/devicelogin and
enter the code XXXXXXXXX to authenticate.
[
  {
    "cloudName": "AzureCloud",
    "id": "***************************",
    "isDefault": true,
    "name": "Free Trial",
    "state": "Enabled",
    "tenantId": "***************************",
    "user": {
      "name": "******@hotmail.com",
      "type": "user"
    }
  }
]
```

Create an Azure resource group named k8s to hold all your AKS resources, such as VMs and networking components, and to make it easy to clean up and tear down later:

```
$ az group create --name k8s --location northeurope
{
  "id": "/subscriptions/**********************/resourceGroups/k8s",
  "location": "northeurope",
  "managedBy": null,
  "name": "k8s",
  "properties": {
    "provisioningState": "Succeeded"
  },
  "tags": null,
  "type": "Microsoft.Resources/resourceGroups"
}
```

If you're unsure what region (*https://oreil.ly/fdGdc*) to use for the --location argument, execute az account list-locations and pick one near you.

Now that you have the resource group k8s set up, you can create the cluster with one worker node (*agent* in Azure terminology), like so:

```
$ az aks create -g k8s -n myAKSCluster --node-count 1 --generate-ssh-keys
{
  "aadProfile": null,
  "addonProfiles": null,
  "agentPoolProfiles": [
    {
      "availabilityZones": null,
      "count": 1,
      "creationData": null,
      "currentOrchestratorVersion": "1.26.6",
```

Note that the `az aks create` command might take several minutes to complete. Once completed, the command returns a JSON object with information about the created cluster.

As a result, in the Azure portal you should see something like Figure 2-5. Start by finding the k8s resource group and then navigate your way to the Deployments tab.

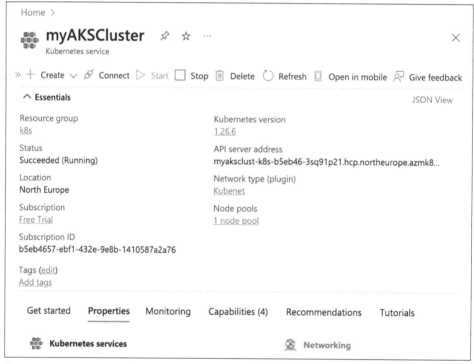

Figure 2-5. Azure portal, showing an AKS cluster in the k8s resource group

You're now in a position to connect to the cluster:

```
$ az aks get-credentials --resource-group k8s --name myAKSCluster
```

You can now poke around in the environment and verify the setup:

```
$ kubectl cluster-info
Kubernetes master is running at https://k8scb-k8s-143f1emgmt.northeurope.cloudapp
  .azure.com
Heapster is running at https://k8scb-k8s-143f1emgmt.northeurope.cloudapp.azure
  .com/api/v1/namespaces/kube-system/services/heapster/proxy
KubeDNS is running at https://k8scb-k8s-143f1emgmt.northeurope.cloudapp.azure
  .com/api/v1/namespaces/kube-system/services/kube-dns/proxy
kubernetes-dashboard is running at https://k8scb-k8s-143f1emgmt.northeurope
  .cloudapp.azure.com/api/v1/namespaces/kube-system/services/kubernetes-dashboard
  /proxy
tiller-deploy is running at https://k8scb-k8s-143f1emgmt.northeurope.cloudapp
  .azure.com/api/v1/namespaces/kube-system/services/tiller-deploy/proxy

To further debug and diagnose cluster problems, use 'kubectl cluster-info dump'.

$ kubectl get nodes
NAME                                STATUS   ROLES   AGE   VERSION
aks-nodepool1-78916010-vmss000000   Ready    agent   26m   v1.24.9
```

Indeed, as you can see from the output, we have created a single-node cluster.

> If you don't want to or cannot install the Azure CLI, an alternative is to use the Azure Cloud Shell (*https://oreil.ly/IUFJQ*) from your browser.

When you're done discovering AKS, don't forget to shut down the cluster and remove all the resources by deleting the resource group k8s:

```
$ az group delete --name k8s --yes --no-wait
```

Although the `az group delete` command returns immediately, due to the presence of the `--no-wait` flag, it can take up to 10 minutes for all the resources to be removed and the resource group to actually be destroyed. You might want to check in the Azure portal to make sure everything went according to plan.

See Also

- "Quickstart: Deploy an Azure Kubernetes Service cluster using Azure CLI" (*https://oreil.ly/YXv3B*) in the Microsoft Azure documentation

2.13 Creating a Kubernetes Cluster on Amazon Elastic Kubernetes Service

Problem

You want to create a Kubernetes cluster on Amazon Elastic Kubernetes Service (EKS).

Solution

To create a cluster in Amazon EKS, you need the following:

- An Amazon Web Services (*https://aws.amazon.com*) account
- AWS CLI (*https://aws.amazon.com/cli*) installed
- eksctl (*https://eksctl.io*) CLI tool installed

After you've installed the AWS CLI, authenticate the client (*https://oreil.ly/_6VMv*) to access your AWS account:

```
$ aws configure
AWS Access Key ID [None]: AKIAIOSFODNN7EXAMPLE
AWS Secret Access Key [None]: wJalrXUtnFEMI/K7MDENG/bPxRfiCYEXAMPLEKEY
Default region name [None]: eu-central-1
Default output format [None]:
```

The eksctl tool is the official CLI for Amazon EKS. It uses the AWS credentials you've configured to authenticate with AWS. Using eksctl, create the cluster:

```
$ eksctl create cluster --name oreilly --region eu-central-1
2023-08-29 13:21:12 [i]  eksctl version 0.153.0-dev+a79b3826a.2023-08-18T...
2023-08-29 13:21:12 [i]  using region eu-central-1
...
2023-08-29 13:36:52 [✔]  EKS cluster "oreilly" in "eu-central-1" region is ready
```

By default, eksctl creates a cluster with two worker nodes in the specified region. You can adjust this paramater by specifying the --nodes flag.

> For the lowest latency, choose the AWS region (*https://oreil.ly/Kc9GZ*) that's nearest to you.

When you no longer need the EKS cluster, delete it to avoid being charged for unused resources:

```
$ eksctl delete cluster oreilly --region eu-central-1
```

See Also

- eksctl Introduction (*https://eksctl.io/getting-started*)
- Amazon Elastic Kubernetes Service (*https://aws.amazon.com/eks*)

## CHAPTER 3

Learning to Use the Kubernetes Client

This chapter gathers recipes around the basic usage of the Kubernetes CLI, kubectl. See Chapter 1 for how to install the CLI tool; for advanced use cases, see Chapter 7, where we show how to use the Kubernetes API.

3.1 Listing Resources

Problem

You want to list Kubernetes resources of a certain kind.

Solution

Use the get verb of kubectl along with the resource type. To list all pods, do this:

```
$ kubectl get pods
```

To list all services and deployments (note that there is no space after the comma), do this:

```
$ kubectl get services,deployments
```

To list a specific deployment, do this:

```
$ kubectl get deployment <deployment-name>
```

To list all resources, do this:

```
$ kubectl get all
```

Note that kubectl get is a very basic but extremely useful command to get a quick overview what is going on in the cluster—it's essentially the equivalent to ps on Unix.

Short Names for Kubernetes Resources

Many resources have short names you can use with kubectl, saving your time and sanity. Here are some examples:

- configmaps (aka cm)
- daemonsets (aka ds)
- deployments (aka deploy)
- endpoints (aka ep)
- events (aka ev)
- horizontalpodautoscalers (aka hpa)
- ingresses (aka ing)
- namespaces (aka ns)
- nodes (aka no)
- persistentvolumeclaims (aka pvc)
- persistentvolumes (aka pv)
- pods (aka po)
- replicasets (aka rs)
- replicationcontrollers (aka rc)
- resourcequotas (aka quota)
- serviceaccounts (aka sa)
- services (aka svc)

Discussion

We strongly recommend enabling autocompletion to avoid having to remember all the Kubernetes resource names. Head to Recipe 12.1 for details on how to do this.

3.2 Deleting Resources

Problem

You no longer need resources and want to get rid of them.

Solution

Use the `delete` verb of `kubectl` along with the type and name of the resource you want to delete.

To delete all resources in the namespace `my-app`, as well as the namespace itself, do this:

```
$ kubectl get ns
NAME          STATUS   AGE
default       Active   2d
kube-public   Active   2d
kube-system   Active   2d
my-app        Active   20m

$ kubectl delete ns my-app
namespace "my-app" deleted
```

Note that you cannot delete the `default` namespace in Kubernetes. This is another reason why it is worth creating your own namespaces, as it can be much easier to clean up the environment. Having said that, you can still delete all objects in a namespace, such as the `default` namespace, with the following command:

```
$ kubectl delete all --all -n <namespace>
```

If you're wondering how to create a namespace, see Recipe 7.3.

You can also delete specific resources and/or influence the process by which they are destroyed. To delete services and deployments labeled with `app=niceone`, do this:

```
$ kubectl delete svc,deploy -l app=niceone
```

To force deletion of a pod named `hangingpod`, do this:

```
$ kubectl delete pod hangingpod --grace-period=0 --force
```

To delete all pods in the namespace `test`, do this:

```
$ kubectl delete pods --all --namespace test
```

Discussion

Do not delete supervised objects such as pods or replica sets that are directly controlled by a deployment. Rather, kill their supervisors or use dedicated operations to get rid of the managed resources. For example, if you scale a deployment to zero replicas (see Recipe 9.1), then you effectively delete all the pods it looks after.

Another aspect to take into account is cascading versus direct deletion—for example, when you delete a custom resource definition (CRD), as shown in Recipe 15.4, all its dependent objects are deleted too. To learn more about how to influence the cascading deletion policy, read Garbage Collection (*https://oreil.ly/8AcpW*) in the Kubernetes documentation.

3.3 Watching Resource Changes with kubectl

Problem

You want to watch the changes to Kubernetes objects in an interactive manner in the terminal.

Solution

The kubectl command has a `--watch` option that gives you this behavior. For example, to watch pods, do this:

```
$ kubectl get pods --watch
```

Note that this is a blocking and auto-updating command, akin to `top`.

Discussion

The `--watch` option is useful, but some prefer the formatting of the output from the `watch` command (*https://oreil.ly/WPueN*), as in:

```
$ watch kubectl get pods
```

3.4 Editing Objects with kubectl

Problem

You want to update the properties of a Kubernetes object.

Solution

Use the `edit` verb of kubectl along with the object type:

```
$ kubectl run nginx --image=nginx
$ kubectl edit pod/nginx
```

Now edit the nginx pod in your editor—for example, add a new label called `mylabel` with the value `true`. Once you save, you'll see something like this:

```
pod/nginx edited
```

Discussion

If your editor isn't opening or you want to specify which editor should be used, set the EDITOR or KUBE_EDITOR environment variable to the name of the editor you'd like to use. For example:

```
$ export EDITOR=vi
```

Also be aware that not all changes trigger an object update.

Some triggers have shortcuts; for example, if you want to change the image version a deployment uses, simply use kubectl set image, which updates the existing container images of resources (valid for deployments, replica sets/replication controllers, daemon sets, jobs, and simple pods).

3.5 Asking kubectl to Explain Resources and Fields

Problem

You want to gain a deeper understanding of a certain resource—for example, a Service—and/or understand what exactly a certain field in a Kubernetes manifest means, including default values and if it's required or optional.

Solution

Use the explain verb of kubectl:

```
$ kubectl explain svc
KIND:       Service
VERSION:    v1

DESCRIPTION:
Service is a named abstraction of software service (for example, mysql)
consisting of local port (for example 3306) that the proxy listens on, and the
selector that determines which pods will answer requests sent through the proxy.

FIELDS:
   status      <Object>
     Most recently observed status of the service. Populated by the system.
     Read-only. More info: https://git.k8s.io/community/contributors/devel/
     api-conventions.md#spec-and-status/

   apiVersion   <string>
     APIVersion defines the versioned schema of this representation of an
     object. Servers should convert recognized schemas to the latest internal
     value, and may reject unrecognized values. More info:
     https://git.k8s.io/community/contributors/devel/api-conventions.md#resources

   kind <string>
```

Kind is a string value representing the REST resource this object
represents. Servers may infer this from the endpoint the client submits
requests to. Cannot be updated. In CamelCase. More info:
https://git.k8s.io/community/contributors/devel/api-conventions
.md#types-kinds

```
metadata    <Object>
  Standard object's metadata. More info:
  https://git.k8s.io/community/contributors/devel/api-conventions.md#metadata

spec <Object>
  Spec defines the behavior of a service. https://git.k8s.io/community/
  contributors/devel/api-conventions.md#spec-and-status/
```

```
$ kubectl explain svc.spec.externalIPs
KIND:       Service
VERSION:    v1

FIELD: externalIPs <[]string>

DESCRIPTION:
     externalIPs is a list of IP addresses for which nodes in the cluster will
     also accept traffic for this service.  These IPs are not managed by
     Kubernetes.  The user is responsible for ensuring that traffic arrives at a
     node with this IP.  A common example is external load-balancers that are not
     part of the Kubernetes system.
```

Discussion

The kubectl explain (*https://oreil.ly/chI_-*) command pulls the descriptions of
resources and fields from the Swagger/OpenAPI definitions (*https://oreil.ly/19vi3*),
exposed by the API server.

You can think of kubectl explain as a way to describe the structure of Kubernetes
resources, whereas kubectl describe is a way to describe the values of objects,
which are instances of those structured resources.

See Also

- Ross Kukulinski's blog post, "kubectl explain—#HeptioProTip" (*https://oreil.ly/
  LulwG*)

## CHAPTER 4

Creating and Modifying Fundamental Workloads

In this chapter, we present recipes that show you how to manage fundamental Kubernetes workload types: pods and deployments. We show how to create deployments and pods via CLI commands and from a YAML manifest and explain how to scale and update a deployment.

4.1 Creating a Pod Using kubectl run

Problem

You want to quickly launch a long-running application such as a web server.

Solution

Use the `kubectl run` command, a generator that creates a pod on the fly. For example, to create a pod that runs the NGINX reverse proxy, do the following:

```
$ kubectl run nginx --image=nginx

$ kubectl get pod/nginx
NAME    READY   STATUS    RESTARTS   AGE
nginx   1/1     Running   0          3m55s
```

Discussion

The kubectl run command can take a number of arguments to configure additional parameters of the pods. For example, you can do the following:

- Set environment variables with --env.
- Define container ports with --port.
- Define a command to run using --command.
- Automatically create an associated service with --expose.
- Test a run without actually running anything with --dry-run=client.

Typical usages are as follows. To launch NGINX serving on port 2368 and create a service along with it, enter the following:

```
$ kubectl run nginx --image=nginx --port=2368 --expose
```

To launch MySQL with the root password set, enter this:

```
$ kubectl run mysql --image=mysql --env=MYSQL_ROOT_PASSWORD=root
```

To launch a busybox container and execute the command sleep 3600 on start, enter this:

```
$ kubectl run myshell --image=busybox:1.36 --command -- sh -c "sleep 3600"
```

See also kubectl run --help for more details about the available arguments.

4.2 Creating a Deployment Using kubectl create

Problem

You want to quickly launch a long-running application such as a content management system.

Solution

Use kubectl create deployment to create a deployment manifest on the fly. For example, to create a deployment that runs the WordPress content management system, do the following:

```
$ kubectl create deployment wordpress --image wordpress:6.3.1

$ kubectl get deployments.apps/wordpress
NAME        READY   UP-TO-DATE   AVAILABLE   AGE
wordpress   1/1     1            1           90s
```

Discussion

The `kubectl create deployment` command can take a number of arguments to configure additional parameters of the deployments. For example, you can do the following:

- Define container ports with `--port`.
- Define the number of replicas using `--replicas`.
- Test a run without actually running anything with `--dry-run=client`.
- Provide the created manifest using `--output yaml`.

See also `kubectl create deployment --help` for more details about the available arguments.

4.3 Creating Objects from File Manifests

Problem

Rather than creating an object via a generator such as `kubectl run`, you want to explicitly state its properties and then create it.

Solution

Use `kubectl apply` like so:

```
$ kubectl apply -f <manifest>
```

In Recipe 7.3 you'll see how to create a namespace using a YAML manifest. This is one of the simplest examples as the manifest is very short. It can be written in YAML or JSON—for example, with a YAML manifest file *myns.yaml* like so:

```
apiVersion: v1
kind: Namespace
metadata:
  name: myns
```

You can create this object with this:

```
$ kubectl apply -f myns.yaml
```

Check that the namespace was created with this:

```
$ kubectl get namespaces
```

Discussion

You can point `kubectl apply` to a URL instead of a filename in your local filesystem. For example, to create the frontend for the canonical Guestbook application, get the URL of the raw YAML that defines the application in a single manifest and enter this:

```
$ kubectl apply -f https://raw.githubusercontent.com/kubernetes/examples/
    master/guestbook/all-in-one/guestbook-all-in-one.yaml
```

Check to see the resources that were created by this operation, for example with this:

```
$ kubectl get all
```

4.4 Writing a Pod Manifest from Scratch

Problem

You want to write a pod manifest from scratch and apply it declaratively, as opposed to using a command like `kubectl run`, which is imperative and does not require manually editing a manifest.

Solution

A pod is an `/api/v1` object, and like any other Kubernetes object, its manifest file contains the following fields:

- `apiVersion`, which specifies the API version
- `kind`, which indicates the type of the object
- `metadata`, which provides some metadata about the object
- `spec`, which provides the object specification

The pod manifest contains an array of containers and an optional array of volumes (see Chapter 8). In its simplest form, with a single container and no volume, it looks something like this:

```
apiVersion: v1
kind: Pod
metadata:
  name: oreilly
spec:
  containers:
  - name: oreilly
    image: nginx:1.25.2
```

Save this YAML manifest in a file called *oreilly.yaml* and then use kubectl to create it:

```
$ kubectl apply -f oreilly.yaml
```

Check to see the resources that were created by this operation, for example with this:

```
$ kubectl get all
```

Discussion

The API specification of a pod is much richer than what is shown in the Solution, which is the most basic functioning pod. For example, a pod can contain multiple containers, as shown here:

```
apiVersion: v1
kind: Pod
metadata:
  name: oreilly
spec:
  containers:
  - name: oreilly
    image: nginx:1.25.2
  - name: safari
    image: redis:7.2.0
```

A pod can also contain volume definitions to load data in the containers (see Recipe 8.1), as well as probes to check the health of the containerized application (see Recipes 11.2 and 11.3).

A description of the thinking behind many of the specification fields and a link to the full API object specification are detailed in the documentation (*https://oreil.ly/pSCBL*).

> Unless for very specific reasons, never create a pod on its own. Use a `Deployment` object (see Recipe 4.5) to supervise pods—it will watch over the pods through another object called a `ReplicaSet`.

4.5 Launching a Deployment Using a Manifest

Problem

You want to have full control over how a (long-running) app is launched and supervised.

Solution

Write a deployment manifest. For the basics, see also Recipe 4.4.

Let's say you have manifest file called *fancyapp.yaml* with the following contents:

```
apiVersion: apps/v1
kind: Deployment
metadata:
  name: fancyapp
spec:
  replicas: 5
  selector:
    matchLabels:
      app: fancy
  template:
    metadata:
      labels:
        app: fancy
        env: development
    spec:
      containers:
      - name: sise
        image: gcr.io/google-samples/hello-app:2.0
        ports:
        - containerPort: 8080
        env:
        - name: SIMPLE_SERVICE_VERSION
          value: "2.0"
```

As you can see, there are a couple of things you might want to do explicitly when launching the app:

- Set the number of pods (`replicas`), or identical copies, that should be launched and supervised.

- Label it, such as with `env=development` (see also Recipes 7.5 and 7.6).

- Set environment variables, such as `SIMPLE_SERVICE_VERSION`.

Now let's look at what the deployment entails:

```
$ kubectl apply -f fancyapp.yaml
deployment.apps/fancyapp created

$ kubectl get deployments
NAME        READY   UP-TO-DATE   AVAILABLE   AGE
fancyapp    5/5     5            5           57s

$ kubectl get replicasets
NAME                   DESIRED   CURRENT   READY   AGE
fancyapp-1223770997    5         5         0       59s
```

```
$ kubectl get pods -l app=fancy
NAME                          READY   STATUS    RESTARTS   AGE
fancyapp-74c6f7cfd7-98d97     1/1     Running   0          115s
fancyapp-74c6f7cfd7-9gm2l     1/1     Running   0          115s
fancyapp-74c6f7cfd7-kggsx     1/1     Running   0          115s
fancyapp-74c6f7cfd7-xfs6v     1/1     Running   0          115s
fancyapp-74c6f7cfd7-xntk2     1/1     Running   0          115s
```

 When you want to get rid of a deployment, and with it the replica sets and pods it supervises, execute a command like kubectl
delete deploy/fancyapp. Do *not* try to delete individual pods, as
they will be re-created by the deployment. This is something that
often confuses beginners.

Deployments allow you to scale the app (see Recipe 9.1) as well as roll out a new
version or roll back a ReplicaSet to a previous version. They are, in general, good for
stateless apps that require pods with identical characteristics.

Discussion

A deployment is a supervisor for pods and replica sets (RSs), giving you fine-grained
control over how and when a new pod version is rolled out or rolled back to a previous state. The RSs and pods that a deployment supervises are generally of no interest
to you unless, for example, you need to debug a pod (see Recipe 12.5). Figure 4-1
illustrates how you can move back and forth between deployment revisions.

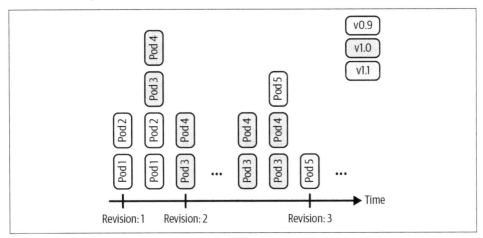

Figure 4-1. Deployment revisions

To generate the manifest for a deployment, you can use the kubectl create command and the --dry-run=client option. This will allow you to generate the manifest
in YAML or JSON format and save the manifest for later use. For example, to create

the manifest of a deployment called `fancy-app` using the container image `nginx`, issue the following command:

```
$ kubectl create deployment fancyapp --image nginx:1.25.2 -o yaml \
    --dry-run=client
kind: Deployment
apiVersion: apps/v1
metadata:
  name: fancyapp
  creationTimestamp:
  labels:
    app: fancyapp
...
```

See Also

- Kubernetes `Deployment` documentation (*https://oreil.ly/IAghn*)

4.6 Updating a Deployment

Problem

You have a deployment and want to roll out a new version of your app.

Solution

Update your deployment and let the default update strategy, `RollingUpdate`, automatically handle the rollout.

For example, if you create a new container image and want to update the deployment based on it, you can do this:

```
$ kubectl create deployment myapp --image=gcr.io/google-samples/hello-app:1.0
deployment.apps/myapp created

$ kubectl set image deployment/myapp \
    hello-app=gcr.io/google-samples/hello-app:2.0
deployment.apps/myapp image updated

$ kubectl rollout status deployment myapp
deployment "myapp" successfully rolled out

$ kubectl rollout history deployment myapp
deployment.apps/myapp
REVISION        CHANGE-CAUSE
1               <none>
2               <none>
```

You've now successfully rolled out a new revision of your deployment where only the container image used has changed. All other properties of the deployment, such as the number of replicas, stay unchanged. But what if you want to update other aspects of the deployment, such as changing environment variables? You can use a number of kubectl commands to update the deployment. For example, to add a port definition to the current deployment, you can use kubectl edit:

```
$ kubectl edit deploy myapp
```

This command will open the current deployment in your default editor or, when set and exported, in the editor specified by the environment variable KUBE_EDITOR.

Say you want to add the following port definition (see Figure 4-2 for the full file):

```
...
  ports:
  - containerPort: 9876
...
```

The result of the editing process (in this case, with KUBE_EDITOR set to vi) is shown in Figure 4-2.

Once you save and exit the editor, Kubernetes kicks off a new deployment, now with the port defined. Let's verify that:

```
$ kubectl rollout history deployment myapp
deployments "sise"
REVISION        CHANGE-CAUSE
1               <none>
2               <none>
3               <none>
```

Indeed, we see that revision 3 has been rolled out with the changes we introduced with kubectl edit. However, the CHANGE-CAUSE column is empty. You can specify a change cause for a revision by using a special annotation. The following is an example of setting a change cause for the most recent revision:

```
$ kubectl annotate deployment/myapp \
    kubernetes.io/change-cause="Added port definition."
deployment.apps/myapp annotate
```

```
# Please edit the object below. Lines beginning with a '#' will be ignored,
# and an empty file will abort the edit. If an error occurs while saving this file will be
# reopened with the relevant failures.
#
apiVersion: apps/v1
kind: Deployment
metadata:
  annotations:
    deployment.kubernetes.io/revision: "2"
  creationTimestamp: "2023-09-13T05:06:27Z"
  generation: 2
  labels:
    app: myapp
  name: myapp
  namespace: default
  resourceVersion: "563"
  uid: e2400f36-0438-43fc-8c28-2201e5661ded
spec:
  progressDeadlineSeconds: 600
  replicas: 1
  revisionHistoryLimit: 10
  selector:
    matchLabels:
      app: myapp
  strategy:
    rollingUpdate:
      maxSurge: 25%
      maxUnavailable: 25%
    type: RollingUpdate
  template:
    metadata:
      creationTimestamp: null
      labels:
        app: myapp
    spec:
      containers:
      - image: gcr.io/google-samples/hello-app:2.0
        imagePullPolicy: IfNotPresent
        name: hello-app
        ports:
        - containerPort: 9876
        resources: {}
        terminationMessagePath: /dev/termination-log
        terminationMessagePolicy: File
      dnsPolicy: ClusterFirst
      restartPolicy: Always
      schedulerName: default-scheduler
      securityContext: {}
      terminationGracePeriodSeconds: 30
-- INSERT --
```

Figure 4-2. Editing a deployment

As mentioned earlier, there are more `kubectl` commands that you can use to update
your deployment:

- Use `kubectl apply` to update a deployment (or create it if it doesn't exist) from a
  manifest file—for example, `kubectl apply -f simpleservice.yaml`.

- Use kubectl `replace` to replace a deployment from a manifest file—for example, kubectl `replace -f simpleservice.yaml`. Note that unlike with `apply`, to use `replace`, the deployment must already exist.

- Use kubectl `patch` to update a specific key—for example:
  ```
  kubectl patch deployment myapp -p '{"spec": {"template":
  {"spec": {"containers":
  [{"name": "sise", "image": "gcr.io/google-samples/hello-app:2.0"}]}}}}'
  ```

What if you make a mistake or experience issues with the new version of the deployment? Luckily, Kubernetes makes it really easy to roll back to a known good state using the kubectl `rollout undo` command. For example, suppose the last edit was a mistake and you want to roll back to revision 2. You can do this with the following command:

```
$ kubectl rollout undo deployment myapp --to-revision 2
```

You can then verify that the port definition has been removed with kubectl `get deploy/myapp -o yaml`.

 The rollout of a deployment is triggered only if parts of the pod template (that is, keys below `.spec.template`) are changed, such as environment variables, ports, or the container image. Changes to aspects of the deployments, such as the replica count, do not trigger a new deployment.

4.7 Running a Batch Job

Problem

You want to run a process that runs for a certain time to completion, such as a batch conversion, backup operation, or database schema upgrade.

Solution

Use a Kubernetes Job (*https://oreil.ly/1whb2*) to launch and supervise the pod(s) that will carry out the batch process.

First, define the Kubernetes manifest for the job in a file called *counter-batch-job.yaml*:

```
apiVersion: batch/v1
kind: Job
metadata:
  name: counter
spec:
  template:
```

```
  metadata:
    name: counter
  spec:
    containers:
    - name: counter
      image: busybox:1.36
      command:
      - "sh"
      - "-c"
      - "for i in 1 2 3 ; do echo $i ; done"
      restartPolicy: Never
```

Then launch the job and take a look at its status:

```
$ kubectl apply -f counter-batch-job.yaml
job.batch/counter created

$ kubectl get jobs
NAME       COMPLETIONS   DURATION   AGE
counter    1/1           7s         12s

$ kubectl describe jobs/counter
Name:            counter
Namespace:       default
Selector:        controller-uid=2d21031e-7263-4ff1-becd-48406393edd5
Labels:          controller-uid=2d21031e-7263-4ff1-becd-48406393edd5
                 job-name=counter
Annotations:     batch.kubernetes.io/job-tracking:
Parallelism:     1
Completions:     1
Completion Mode: NonIndexed
Start Time:      Mon, 03 Apr 2023 18:19:13 +0530
Completed At:    Mon, 03 Apr 2023 18:19:20 +0530
Duration:        7s
Pods Statuses:   0 Active (0 Ready) / 1 Succeeded / 0 Failed
Pod Template:
  Labels:  controller-uid=2d21031e-7263-4ff1-becd-48406393edd5
           job-name=counter
  Containers:
   counter:
    Image:       busybox:1.36
    Port:        <none>
    Host Port:   <none>
    Command:
      sh
      -c
      for i in 1 2 3 ; do echo $i ; done
    Environment:  <none>
    Mounts:       <none>
  Volumes:        <none>
Events:
  Type    Reason        Age    From        Message
  ----    ------        ----   ----        -------
```

```
Normal  SuccessfulCreate  30s   job-controller  Created pod: counter-5c8s5
Normal  Completed         23s   job-controller  Job completed
```

Finally, you want to verify that it actually carried out the task (counting from 1 to 3):

```
$ kubectl logs jobs/counter
1
2
3
```

Indeed, as you can see, the `counter` job counted as expected.

Discussion

After a job has executed successfully, the pod that was created by the job will be in the *Completed* state. You can delete the job if you don't need it anymore, which will clean up the pods it created:

```
$ kubectl delete jobs/counter
```

You can also temporarily suspend a job's execution and resume it later. Suspending a job will also clean up the pods it created:

```
$ kubectl patch jobs/counter --type=strategic --patch '{"spec":{"suspend":true}}'
```

To resume the job, simply flip the `suspend` flag:

```
$ kubectl patch jobs/counter --type=strategic \
    --patch '{"spec":{"suspend":false}}'
```

4.8 Running a Task on a Schedule Within a Pod

Problem

You want to run a task on a specific schedule within a pod managed by Kubernetes.

Solution

Use Kubernetes `CronJob` objects. The `CronJob` object is a derivative of the more generic `Job` object (see Recipe 4.7).

You can periodically schedule a job by writing a manifest similar to the one shown here. In the `spec`, you see a `schedule` section that follows the crontab format. You can also use some macros, such as `@hourly`, `@daily`, `@weekly`, `@monthly`, and `@yearly`. The `template` section describes the pod that will run and the command that will get executed (this one prints the current date and time every hour to `stdout`):

```
apiVersion: batch/v1
kind: CronJob
metadata:
  name: hourly-date
```

```
spec:
  schedule: "0 * * * *"
  jobTemplate:
    spec:
      template:
        spec:
          containers:
          - name: date
            image: busybox:1.36
            command:
              - "sh"
              - "-c"
              - "date"
          restartPolicy: OnFailure
```

Discussion

Just like a job, a cron job can be also be suspended and resumed by flipping the suspend flag. For example:

```
$ kubectl patch cronjob.batch/hourly-date --type=strategic \
    --patch '{"spec":{"suspend":true}}'
```

If you don't need the cron job anymore, delete it to clean up the pods that it created:

```
$ kubectl delete cronjob.batch/hourly-date
```

See Also

- Kubernetes `CronJob` documentation (*https://oreil.ly/nrxxh*)

4.9 Running Infrastructure Daemons per Node

Problem

You want to launch an infrastructure daemon—for example, a log collector or monitoring agent—making sure that exactly one pod runs per node.

Solution

Use a `DaemonSet` to launch and supervise the daemon process. For example, to launch a Fluentd agent on each node in your cluster, create a file named *fluentd-daemonset.yaml* with the following contents:

```
kind: DaemonSet
apiVersion: apps/v1
metadata:
  name: fluentd
spec:
```

```
  selector:
    matchLabels:
      app: fluentd
  template:
    metadata:
      labels:
        app: fluentd
      name: fluentd
    spec:
      containers:
      - name: fluentd
        image: gcr.io/google_containers/fluentd-elasticsearch:1.3
        env:
         - name: FLUENTD_ARGS
           value: -qq
        volumeMounts:
        - name: varlog
          mountPath: /varlog
        - name: containers
          mountPath: /var/lib/docker/containers
      volumes:
        - hostPath:
            path: /var/log
          name: varlog
        - hostPath:
            path: /var/lib/docker/containers
          name: containers
```

Now launch the DaemonSet, like so:

```
$ kubectl apply -f fluentd-daemonset.yaml
daemonset.apps/fluentd created

$ kubectl get ds
NAME      DESIRED   CURRENT   READY   UP-TO-DATE   AVAILABLE   NODE SELECTOR   AGE
fluentd   1         1         1       1            1           <none>          60s

$ kubectl describe ds/fluentd
Name:           fluentd
Selector:       app=fluentd
Node-Selector:  <none>
Labels:         <none>
Annotations:    deprecated.daemonset.template.generation: 1
Desired Number of Nodes Scheduled: 1
Current Number of Nodes Scheduled: 1
Number of Nodes Scheduled with Up-to-date Pods: 1
Number of Nodes Scheduled with Available Pods: 1
Number of Nodes Misscheduled: 0
Pods Status:  1 Running / 0 Waiting / 0 Succeeded / 0 Failed
...
```

Discussion

Note that in the preceding output, because the command is executed on Minikube, you see only one pod running as there's only one node in this setup. If you had 15 nodes in your cluster, you'd have 15 pods overall with 1 pod per node running. You can also restrict the daemon to certain nodes using the `nodeSelector` section in the `spec` of the `DaemonSet` manifest.

## CHAPTER 5

Working with Services

In this chapter, we discuss how pods communicate within the cluster, how applications discover each other, and how to expose pods so that they can be accessed from outside of the cluster.

The resource we will be using here is called a Kubernetes *service* (*https://oreil.ly/BGn9e*), as depicted in Figure 5-1.

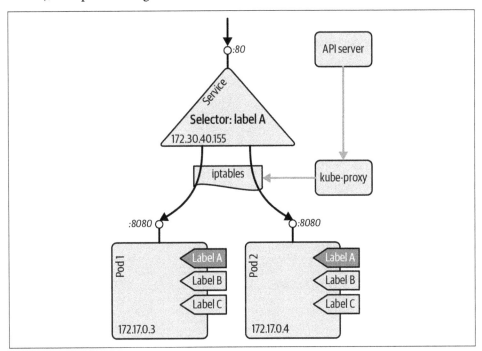

Figure 5-1. The Kubernetes service concept

A service provides a stable virtual IP (VIP) address for a set of pods. Though pods may come and go, services allow clients to reliably discover and connect to the containers running in the pods by using the VIP. The "virtual" in VIP means it's not an actual IP address connected to a network interface; its purpose is purely to forward traffic to one or more pods. Keeping the mapping between the VIPs and the pods up to date is the job of kube-proxy, a process that runs on every node on the cluster. This kube-proxy process queries the API server to learn about new services in the cluster and updates the node's iptables rules (iptables) accordingly to provide the necessary routing information.

5.1 Creating a Service to Expose Your Application

Problem

You want to provide a stable and reliable way to discover and access your application within the cluster.

Solution

Create a Kubernetes service for the pods that make up your application.

Assuming you created an nginx deployment with kubectl create deployment nginx --image nginx:1.25.2, you can automatically create a Service object using the kubectl expose command, like so:

```
$ kubectl expose deploy/nginx --port 80
service "nginx" exposed

$ kubectl describe svc/nginx
Name:              nginx
Namespace:         default
Labels:            app=nginx
Annotations:       <none>
Selector:          app=nginx
Type:              ClusterIP
IP Family Policy:  SingleStack
IP Families:       IPv4
IP:                10.97.137.240
IPs:               10.97.137.240
Port:              <unset>  80/TCP
TargetPort:        80/TCP
Endpoints:         172.17.0.3:80
Session Affinity:  None
Events:            <none>
```

You will then see the object appear when you list the `Service`:

```
$ kubectl get svc nginx
NAME      TYPE        CLUSTER-IP     EXTERNAL-IP   PORT(S)   AGE
nginx     ClusterIP   10.97.137.240  <none>        80/TCP    2s
```

Discussion

To access this service via your browser, run a proxy in a separate terminal, like so:

```
$ kubectl proxy
Starting to serve on 127.0.0.1:8001
```

Then open your browser with this:

```
$ open http://localhost:8001/api/v1/namespaces/default/services/nginx/proxy/
```

You should see the NGINX default page.

> If your service does not seem to be working properly, check the labels used in the selector and verify that a set of endpoints is being populated with `kubectl get endpoints <service-name>`. If not, this most likely means that your selector is not finding any matching pods.

If you wanted to create a `Service` object by hand for the same `nginx` deployment, you would write the following YAML file:

```yaml
apiVersion: v1
kind: Service
metadata:
  name: nginx
spec:
  selector:
    app: nginx
  ports:
  - port: 80
```

The one thing to pay attention to in this YAML file is the *selector*, which is used to select all the pods that make up this microservice abstraction. Kubernetes uses the `Service` object to dynamically configure the iptables on all the nodes to be able to send the network traffic to the containers that make up the microservice. The selection is done as a label query (see Recipe 7.6) and results in a list of endpoints.

> Pod supervisors, such as `Deployments` or `ReplicationSets`, operate orthogonally to `Services`. Both supervisors and `Services` find the pods they're looking after by using labels, but they have different jobs to do: supervisors monitor the health of and restart pods, and `Services` make them accessible in a reliable way.

See Also

- Kubernetes `Service` documentation (*https://oreil.ly/BGn9e*)
- Kubernetes tutorial "Using a Service to Expose Your App" (*https://oreil.ly/NVOhU*)

5.2 Verifying the DNS Entry of a Service

Problem

You have created a service (see Recipe 5.1) and want to verify that your Domain Name System (DNS) registration is working properly.

Solution

By default Kubernetes uses `ClusterIP` as the service type, and that exposes the service on a cluster-internal IP. If the DNS cluster add-on is available and working properly, you can access the service via a fully qualified domain name (FQDN) in the form of `$SERVICENAME.$NAMESPACE.svc.cluster.local`.

To verify that this is working as expected, get an interactive shell within a container in your cluster. The easiest way to do this is to use `kubectl run` with the busybox image, like so:

```
$ kubectl run busybox --rm -it --image busybox:1.36 -- /bin/sh
If you don't see a command prompt, try pressing enter.

/ # nslookup nginx
Server:         10.96.0.10
Address:        10.96.0.10:53

Name:   nginx.default.svc.cluster.local
Address: 10.100.34.223
```

The IP address returned for the service should correspond to its cluster IP.

Type `exit` and hit Enter to leave the container.

Discussion

By default, a DNS query will be scoped to the same namespace as the pod making the request. If, in the previous example, you run the busybox pod in a different namespace from the one running `nginx`, by default the lookup won't return any results. To specify the correct namespace, use the syntax *<service-name>.<namespace>*; for example, `nginx.staging`.

5.3 Changing the Type of a Service

Problem

You have an existing service, say of type ClusterIP, as discussed in Recipe 5.2, and you want to change its type so that you can expose your application as a NodePort or via a cloud provider load balancer using the LoadBalancer service type.

Solution

Use the kubectl edit command along with your preferred editor to change the service type. Suppose you have a manifest file called *simple-nginx-svc.yaml* with this content:

```
kind: Service
apiVersion: v1
metadata:
  name: webserver
spec:
  ports:
  - port: 80
  selector:
    app: nginx
```

Create the webserver service and query for it:

```
$ kubectl apply -f simple-nginx-svc.yaml

$ kubectl get svc/webserver
NAME        TYPE        CLUSTER-IP      EXTERNAL-IP   PORT(S)   AGE
webserver   ClusterIP   10.98.223.206   <none>        80/TCP    11s
```

Next, change the service type to, say, NodePort, like so:

```
$ kubectl edit svc/webserver
```

This command will download the current spec the API server has of the service and open it in your default editor. Notice the area in bold toward the end, where we've changed the type from ClusterIP to NodePort:

```
# Please edit the object below. Lines beginning with a '#' will be ignored,
# and an empty file will abort the edit. If an error occurs while saving this...
# reopened with the relevant failures.
#
apiVersion: v1
kind: Service
metadata:
  annotations:
    kubectl.kubernetes.io/last-applied-configuration: |
      {"apiVersion":"v1","kind":"Service","metadata":{"annotations":{},"name"...
  creationTimestamp: "2023-03-01T14:07:55Z"
```

```
  name: webserver
  namespace: default
  resourceVersion: "1128"
  uid: 48daed0e-a16f-4923-bd7e-1d879dc2221f
spec:
  clusterIP: 10.98.223.206
  clusterIPs:
  - 10.98.223.206
  externalTrafficPolicy: Cluster
  internalTrafficPolicy: Cluster
  ipFamilies:
  - IPv4
  ipFamilyPolicy: SingleStack
  ports:
  - nodePort: 31275
    port: 80
    protocol: TCP
    targetPort: 80
  selector:
    app: nginx
  sessionAffinity: None
  type: NodePort
status:
  loadBalancer: {}
```

Once you've saved the edits (changing `type` to `NodePort`), you can verify the updated service, like so:

```
$ kubectl get svc/webserver
NAME         TYPE       CLUSTER-IP      EXTERNAL-IP   PORT(S)       AGE
webserver    NodePort   10.98.223.206   <none>        80:31275/TCP  4m

$ kubectl get svc/webserver -o yaml
apiVersion: v1
kind: Service
metadata:
  annotations:
    kubectl.kubernetes.io/last-applied-configuration: |
      {"apiVersion":"v1","kind":"Service","metadata":{"annotations":{},"name"...
  creationTimestamp: "2023-03-01T14:07:55Z"
  name: webserver
  namespace: default
  resourceVersion: "1128"
  uid: 48daed0e-a16f-4923-bd7e-1d879dc2221f
spec:
  clusterIP: 10.98.223.206
  clusterIPs:
  - 10.98.223.206
  externalTrafficPolicy: Cluster
  internalTrafficPolicy: Cluster
  ipFamilies:
  - IPv4
  ipFamilyPolicy: SingleStack
```

```
  ports:
  - nodePort: 31275
    port: 80
    protocol: TCP
    targetPort: 80
  selector:
    app: nginx
  sessionAffinity: None
  type: NodePort
status:
  loadBalancer: {}
```

Discussion

Note that you can change the service type to whatever suits your use case; however, be aware of the implications of certain types, like `LoadBalancer`, which may trigger the provisioning of public cloud infrastructure components that can be costly if used without awareness and/or monitoring.

See Also

- Details on the different types of Kubernetes services (*https://oreil.ly/r63eA*)

5.4 Deploying an Ingress Controller

Problem

You want to deploy an ingress controller to learn about `Ingress` objects. `Ingress` objects are of interest to you because you want to provide access to your applications running in Kubernetes from outside your Kubernetes cluster; however, you do not want to create a `NodePort`- or `LoadBalancer`-type service.

Solution

An ingress controller acts as a reverse proxy and load balancer. It routes traffic from outside the cluster and load-balances it to the pods running inside the platform, allowing you deploy multiple applications on the cluster, each addressable by hostname and/or URI path.

For `Ingress` objects (discussed in Recipe 5.5) to take effect and provide a route from outside the cluster to your pods, you need to deploy an ingress controller:

```
$ kubectl apply -f https://raw.githubusercontent.com/kubernetes/ingress-nginx/
controller-v1.8.1/deploy/static/provider/cloud/deploy.yaml
```

On Minikube, you can simply enable the `ingress` add-on like so:

```
$ minikube addons enable ingress
```

After a minute or less, a new pod will start in the newly created `ingress-nginx` namespace:

```
$ kubectl get pods -n ingress-nginx
NAME                                        READY  STATUS     RESTARTS  AGE
ingress-nginx-admission-create-xpqbt        0/1    Completed  0         3m39s
ingress-nginx-admission-patch-r7cnf         0/1    Completed  1         3m39s
ingress-nginx-controller-6cc5ccb977-l9hvz   1/1    Running    0         3m39s
```

You are now ready to create `Ingress` objects.

Discussion

NGINX is one of the ingress controllers officially supported by the Kubernetes project, but there are many other open source and commercial solutions (*https://oreil.ly/eukmq*) that support the ingress specification, many of which provide broader API management capabilities.

At the time of writing, the new Kubernetes Gateway API specification (*https://oreil.ly/Y27m-*) is emerging as a future replacement for the ingress specification and is already supported by many third-party gateway providers. If you are just starting out with ingress, it is worth considering the Gateway API as a more future-proof starting point.

See Also

- Kubernetes `Ingress` documentation (*https://oreil.ly/9xoks*)
- NGINX-based ingress controller (*https://oreil.ly/691Lx*)
- Minikube's `ingress-dns` add-on (*https://oreil.ly/To14r*)

5.5 Making Services Accessible from Outside the Cluster

Problem

You want to access a Kubernetes service by URI path from outside of the cluster.

Solution

Use an ingress controller (see Recipe 5.4), configured by creating `Ingress` objects.

Suppose you want to deploy a simple service that can be invoked and returns "Hello, world!" Start by creating the deployment:

```
$ kubectl create deployment web --image=gcr.io/google-samples/hello-app:2.0
```

Then expose the service:

```
$ kubectl expose deployment web --port=8080
```

Verify that all these resources were correctly created with the following:

```
$ kubectl get all -l app=web
NAME                          READY   STATUS    RESTARTS   AGE
pod/web-79b7b8f988-95tjv      1/1     Running   0          47s

NAME          TYPE        CLUSTER-IP       EXTERNAL-IP   PORT(S)    AGE
service/web   ClusterIP   10.100.87.233    <none>        8080/TCP   8s

NAME                    READY   UP-TO-DATE   AVAILABLE   AGE
deployment.apps/web     1/1     1            1           47s

NAME                                DESIRED   CURRENT   READY   AGE
replicaset.apps/web-79b7b8f988      1         1         1       47s
```

The following is the manifest of an `Ingress` object that configures the URI path /web to the `hello-app` service:

```
$ cat nginx-ingress.yaml
apiVersion: networking.k8s.io/v1
kind: Ingress
metadata:
  name: nginx-public
  annotations:
    nginx.ingress.kubernetes.io/rewrite-target: /
spec:
  ingressClassName: nginx
  rules:
  - host:
    http:
      paths:
      - path: /web
        pathType: Prefix
        backend:
          service:
            name: web
            port:
              number: 8080
```

```
$ kubectl apply -f nginx-ingress.yaml
```

Now you can see the `Ingress` object created for NGINX in your Kubernetes dashboard (Figure 5-2).

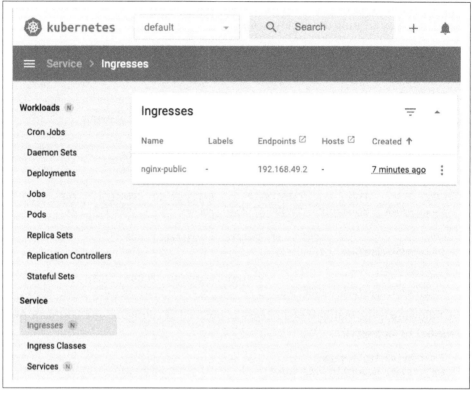

Figure 5-2. NGINX `Ingress` object

From the Kubernetes dashboard, you can see that NGINX will be available via the IP address 192.168.49.2 (yours may differ). Based on this information, you can access NGINX from outside the cluster at the /web URI path as follows:

```
$ curl https://192.168.49.2/web
Hello, world!
Version: 1.0.0
Hostname: web-68487bc957-v9fj8
```

Known Issue with Minikube

Because of known networking limitations when using Minikube with the Docker driver (for example with Docker Desktop), you might not be able to access your service externally using the IP address provided by the `Ingress` object, as shown earlier. In this case, the recommended work-around is to create a tunnel to the cluster using the `minikube service` command. For instance, to expose the service `web` that we created in this recipe, use the following command:

```
$ minikube service web
```

By default this command will open the service in your default browser. Append the `--url` option, and the tunnel URL will be printed out in the terminal. Note that the `minikube service` command will block your terminal while it runs, so we recommend that you run it in a dedicated terminal window.

In the Minikube documentation (*https://oreil.ly/2V4Ln*) you can read more about this limitation.

Discussion

An alternative to using the dashboard to see your service IPs is to use the following command:

```
$ kubectl describe ingress
```

In general, ingress works as depicted in Figure 5-3: the ingress controller listens to the `/ingresses` endpoint of the API server, learning about new rules. It then configures the routes so that external traffic lands at a specific (cluster-internal) service—`service1` on port 9876 in the depicted example.

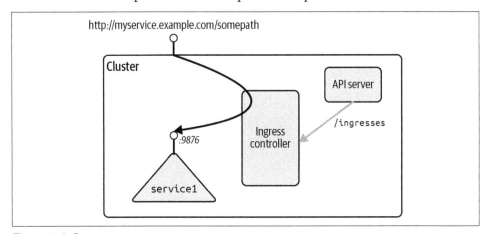

Figure 5-3. Ingress concept

See Also

- The *kubernetes/ingress-nginx* repo on GitHub (*https://oreil.ly/guulG*)

## CHAPTER 6

Managing Application Manifests

In this chapter, we take a look at ways to simplify the management of applications on Kubernetes with the use of tools such as Helm, kompose, and kapp. These tools primarily focus on managing your YAML manifests. Helm is a YAML templating, packaging, and deployment tool, whereas Kompose is a tool that assists you with migrating your Docker Compose files to Kubernetes resource manifests. kapp is a relatively new tool that allows you to manage a group of YAML files as an application and thereby manage their deployment as a single application.

6.1 Installing Helm, the Kubernetes Package Manager

Problem

You do not want to write all your Kubernetes manifests by hand. Instead, you want to be able to search for a package in a repository and download and install it with a command-line interface.

Solution

Use Helm (*https://helm.sh*). Helm consists of a client-side CLI called helm and is used to search for and deploy charts on a Kubernetes cluster.

You can download Helm from the GitHub release page (*https://oreil.ly/0A7Ty*) and move the helm binary into your $PATH. For example, on macOS (Intel), for the v3.12.3 release, do this:

```
$ wget https://get.helm.sh/helm-v3.12.3-darwin-amd64.tar.gz
$ tar -xvf helm-v3.12.3-darwin-amd64.tar.gz
$ sudo mv darwin-amd64/helm /usr/local/bin
```

Alternatively, you can use the handy installer script (*https://oreil.ly/V6_bt*) to install the latest version of Helm:

```
$ wget -O get_helm.sh https://raw.githubusercontent.com/helm/helm/main/
scripts/get-helm-3
```

```
$ chmod +x get_helm.sh
$ ./get_helm.sh
```

Discussion

Helm is the Kubernetes package manager; it defines a Kubernetes package as a set of manifests and some metadata. The manifests are actually templates. The values in the templates are filled when the package is instantiated by Helm. A Helm package is called a *chart*, and packaged charts are made available to users in chart repositories.

Another method of installing Helm on Linux or macOS is to use the Homebrew (*https://brew.sh*) package manager:

```
$ brew install helm
```

6.2 Adding Chart Repositories to Helm

Problem

You've installed the `helm` client (see Recipe 6.1), and now you want to find and add chart repositories to Helm.

Solution

A chart repository consists of packaged charts and some metadata that enables Helm to search for charts in the repository. Before you can begin installing an application with Helm, you need to find and add the chart repository that provides the chart.

As illustrated in Figure 6-1, Artifact Hub (*https://artifacthub.io*) is a web-based service that allows you to search more than 10,000 charts (*https://oreil.ly/0olJi*) from various publishers and add chart repositories to Helm.

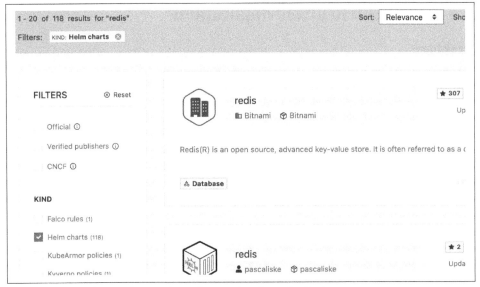

Figure 6-1. Artifact Hub, searching for a Helm chart for Redis

Discussion

The `helm` command also integrates with Artifact Hub, which allows you to search Artifact Hub directly from the `helm` command line.

Let's assume you would like to search for a publisher that provides a Redis chart. You can use the `helm search hub` command to find one:

```
$ helm search hub --list-repo-url redis
URL                     CHART VER... APP VER... DESCRIPTION    REPO URL
https://art...s/redis   0.1.1        6.0.8.9    A Helm cha...  https://spy8...
https://art...s-arm/... 17.8.0       7.0.8      Redis(R) i...  https://libr...
https://art...ontain... 0.15.2       0.15.0     Provides e...  https://ot-c...
...
```

If you want to deploy the chart published by Bitnami (*https://oreil.ly/jL7Xz*), a well-known publisher of more than 100 production-quality charts, add the chart repository using the following:

```
$ helm repo add bitnami https://charts.bitnami.com/bitnami
```

You're all set now to install charts from the repository.

6.3 Using Helm to Install Applications

Problem

You've added a chart repository to Helm (see Recipe 6.2), and now you want to search for charts and deploy them.

Solution

Let's assume you want to deploy the Redis chart from the Bitnami chart repository (*https://oreil.ly/TAPRO*).

Before you search a chart repository, it's a good practice to update the locally cached index of the chart repositories:

```
$ helm repo update
Hang tight while we grab the latest from your chart repositories...
...Successfully got an update from the "bitnami" chart repository
Update Complete. ❀Happy Helming!❀
```

Search for `redis` in the Bitnami chart repository:

```
$ helm search repo bitnami/redis
NAME                   CHART VERSION APP VERSION DESCRIPTION
bitnami/redis          18.0.1        7.2.0       Redis(R) is an...
bitnami/redis-cluster  9.0.1         7.2.0       Redis(R) is an...
```

And use `helm install` to deploy the chart:

```
$ helm install redis bitnami/redis
```

Helm will use the default chart configuration and create a Helm release named `redis`. A Helm release is the collection of all Kubernetes objects defined in a chart that you can manage as a single unit.

After a while you should see the `redis` pods running:

```
$ kubectl get all -l app.kubernetes.io/name=redis
NAME                   READY   STATUS    RESTARTS   AGE
pod/redis-master-0     1/1     Running   0          114s
pod/redis-replicas-0   1/1     Running   0          114s
pod/redis-replicas-1   1/1     Running   0          66s
pod/redis-replicas-2   1/1     Running   0          38s

NAME                     TYPE        CLUSTER-IP      EXTERNAL-IP   PORT(S)    AGE
service/redis-headless   ClusterIP   None            <none>        6379/TCP   114s
service/redis-master     ClusterIP   10.105.20.184   <none>        6379/TCP   114s
service/redis-replicas   ClusterIP   10.105.27.109   <none>        6379/TCP   114s

NAME                              READY   AGE
statefulset.apps/redis-master    1/1     114s
statefulset.apps/redis-replicas  3/3     114s
```

Discussion

The output of the `helm install` command could contain important information about the deployment, such as passwords retrieved from secrets, deployed services, etc. You can use the `helm list` command to list existing helm installations, and then `helm status <name>` to view the details of that installation:

```
% helm status redis
NAME: redis
LAST DEPLOYED: Fri Nov 10 09:42:17 2023
NAMESPACE: default
STATUS: deployed
...
```

To learn more about Helm charts and how to create your own charts, see Recipe 6.8.

6.4 Inspecting the Customizable Parameters of a Chart

Problem

You want to know the customizable parameters of a chart and their default values.

Solution

Chart publishers expose various parameters of a chart that can be configured while installing the chart. The default values of these parameters are configured in a *Values* file whose contents can be viewed using the `helm show values` command—for example:

```
$ helm show values bitnami/redis
...
...
## @param architecture Redis® architecture. Allowed values: `standalone` or
`replication`
##
architecture: replication
...
...
```

Discussion

It's a common practice for publishers to document chart parameters in the *Values* file. However, a chart's *Readme* file can provide more extensive documentation of the various parameters, along with specific usage instructions. To view a chart's *Readme* file, use the `helm show readme` command. For example:

```
$ helm show readme bitnami/redis
...
...
### Redis® common configuration parameters

| Name            | Description                     | Value          |
| --------------- | ------------------------------- | -------------- |
| `architecture`  | Redis® architecture...          | `replication`  |
| `auth.enabled`  | Enable password authentication  | `true`         |
...
...
```

It's worth noting that this *Readme* is the same as the one rendered for the chart on Artifact Hub (*https://oreil.ly/dIYpI*).

6.5 Overriding Chart Parameters

Problem

You've learned about the various customizable parameters of a chart (see Recipe 6.4), and now you want to customize the chart deployment.

Solution

The default parameters of a Helm chart can be overridden by passing the `--set` *key=value* flag while installing the chart. The flag can be specified multiple times, or you can separate key/value pairs with commas like so: key1=value1,key2=value2.

For example, you can override the deployment configuration of the `bitnami/redis` chart to use the `standalone` architecture as follows:

```
$ helm install redis bitnami/redis --set architecture=standalone
```

Discussion

When overriding many chart parameters, you can provide the `--values` flag to input a YAML-formatted file with all the parameters you want to override. For the previous example, create a file named *values.yaml* containing this line:

```
architecture: standalone
```

Then input the file to `helm install`:

```
$ helm install redis bitnami/redis --values values.yaml
```

The `standalone` configuration of the `bitnami/redis` chart spawns fewer pod resources and is suitable for development purposes. Let's take a look:

```
$ kubectl get pods
NAME             READY   STATUS    RESTARTS   AGE
redis-master-0   1/1     Running   0          3m14s
```

6.6 Getting the User-Supplied Parameters of a Helm Release

Problem

Your Kubernetes cluster has a Helm release, and you want to know the user-supplied chart parameters that were specified when the chart was installed.

Solution

The `helm list` command gets the list of Helm release objects present in the cluster:

```
$ helm list
NAME   NAMESPACE REVISION  UPDATED            STATUS     CHART         APP VERSION
redis default   1         2022-12-30 14:02... deployed   redis-17.4.0  7.0.7
```

You can get extended information about a Helm release, such as the user-supplied values, using the `helm get` command:

```
$ helm get values redis
USER-SUPPLIED VALUES:
architecture: standalone
```

Discussion

In addition to the `values`, you can also retrieve the YAML manifests, post-deployment notes, and the hooks configured in the chart using the `helm get` command.

6.7 Uninstalling Applications with Helm

Problem

You no longer want an application that was installed using Helm (see Recipe 6.3) and want to remove it.

Solution

When you install an application using a chart, it creates a Helm release that can be managed as a single unit. To remove an application that was installed using Helm, all you need to do is remove the *release* using the `helm uninstall` command.

Let's assume you want to remove a Helm release named *redis*:

```
$ helm uninstall redis
release "redis" uninstalled
```

Helm will remove all the Kubernetes objects associated with the release and free up the cluster resources associated with their objects.

6.8 Creating Your Own Chart to Package Your Application with Helm

Problem

You have written an application with multiple Kubernetes manifests and want to package it as a Helm chart.

Solution

Use the `helm create` and `helm package` commands.

With `helm create`, generate the skeleton of your chart. Issue the command in your terminal, specifying the name of your chart. For example, to create an `oreilly` chart:

```
$ helm create oreilly
Creating oreilly

$ tree oreilly/
oreilly/
├── Chart.yaml
├── charts
├── templates
│   ├── NOTES.txt
│   ├── _helpers.tpl
│   ├── deployment.yaml
│   ├── hpa.yaml
│   ├── ingress.yaml
│   ├── service.yaml
│   ├── serviceaccount.yaml
│   └── tests
│       └── test-connection.yaml
└── values.yaml

3 directories, 10 files
```

Discussion

The `helm create` command generates a scaffolding for a typical web application. You can edit the generated scaffolding and adapt it for your application, or if you have your manifests already written, you can delete the contents of the *templates/* directory and copy your existing templates into it. If you want to templatize your manifests, then write the values that need to be substituted in the manifests in the *values.yaml* file. Edit the metadata file *Chart.yaml*, and if you have any dependent charts, put them in the */charts* directory.

You can test your chart locally by running this:

```
$ helm install oreilly-app ./oreilly
```

Finally, you can package it with `helm package oreilly/` to generate a redistributable tarball of your chart. If you want to publish the chart to a chart repository, copy it to the repository and generate a new *index.yaml* using the command `helm repo index ..`. After the updates to the chart registry are completed, and provided that you have added the chart repository to Helm (see Recipe 6.2), `helm search repo oreilly` should return your chart:

```
$ helm search repo oreilly
NAME                    VERSION DESCRIPTION
oreilly/oreilly         0.1.0   A Helm chart for Kubernetes
```

See Also

- "Create Your First Helm Chart" (*https://oreil.ly/fGfgF*) in the VMware Application Catalog docs
- "The Chart Best Practices Guide" (*https://oreil.ly/kcznF*) in the Helm docs

6.9 Installing Kompose

Problem

You've started using containers with Docker and written some Docker compose files to define your multicontainer application. Now you want to start using Kubernetes and wonder if and how you can reuse your Docker compose files.

Solution

Use Kompose (*https://kompose.io*). Kompose is a tool that converts Docker compose files into Kubernetes (or OpenShift) manifests.

To start, download `kompose` from the GitHub release page (*https://oreil.ly/lmiCJ*) and move it to your $PATH, for convenience.

For example, on macOS, do the following:

```
$ wget https://github.com/kubernetes/kompose/releases/download/v1.27.0/
kompose-darwin-amd64 -O kompose

$ sudo install -m 755 kompose /usr/local/bin/kompose
$ kompose version
```

Alternatively, Linux and macOS users can install the kompose CLI using the Home-brew (*https://brew.sh*) package manager:

```
$ brew install kompose
```

6.10 Converting Your Docker Compose Files to Kubernetes Manifests

Problem

You've installed the kompose command (see Recipe 6.9), and now you want to convert your Docker compose file into Kubernetes manifests.

Solution

Suppose you have the following Docker compose file that starts a redis container:

```
version: '2'

services:
  redis:
    image: redis:7.2.0
    ports:
    - "6379:6379"
```

Using Kompose, you can automatically convert this into Kubernetes manifests with the following command:

```
$ kompose convert
```

Kompose will read the contents of the Docker compose file and generate the Kubernetes manifests in the current directory. Then you can use kubectl apply to create these resources in your cluster.

Discussion

Adding the --stdout argument to the kompose convert command will generate the YAML, which can be directly piped to kubectl apply like so:

```
$ kompose convert --stdout | kubectl apply -f -
```

Some Docker compose directives are not converted to Kubernetes. In this case, kompose prints out a warning informing you that the conversion did not happen.

While in general it doesn't cause problems, it is possible that the conversion may not result in a working manifest in Kubernetes. This is expected, as this type of transformation cannot be perfect. However, it will get you close to a working Kubernetes manifest. Most notably, handling volumes and network isolation will typically require manual, custom work from your side.

6.11 Converting Your Docker Compose File to a Helm Chart

Problem

You've installed the kompose command (see Recipe 6.9), and now you want to create a Helm chart from your Docker compose file.

Solution

As well as using Kompose to convert your Docker compose files to Kubernetes manifests (see Recipe 6.10), you can also use it to generate a Helm chart for the converted objects.

Generate a Helm chart from your Docker compose file using Kompose like so:

```
$ kompose convert --chart
```

A new Helm chart will be generated in the current directory. This chart can be packaged, deployed, and managed using the helm CLI (see Recipe 6.3).

6.12 Installing kapp

Problem

You have written the YAML files to deploy your application to the cluster and want to deploy and manage the lifecycle of the deployment, but you don't want to package it as a Helm chart.

Solution

Use kapp (*https://carvel.dev/kapp*), which is a CLI tool that enables you to manage resources in bulk. Unlike Helm, kapp considers YAML templating outside of its scope and focuses on managing application deployments.

To install kapp, use the download script (*https://oreil.ly/iAQPd*) to download the latest version for your platform from the GitHub release page (*https://oreil.ly/9g2f3*):

```
$ mkdir local-bin/
$ wget https://carvel.dev/install.sh -qO - | \
    K14SIO_INSTALL_BIN_DIR=local-bin bash

$ sudo install -m 755 local-bin/kapp /usr/local/bin/kapp
$ kapp version
```

Discussion

Linux and macOS users can also install kapp using the Homebrew (*https://brew.sh*) package manager:

```
$ brew tap vmware-tanzu/carvel
$ brew install kapp
$ kapp version
```

6.13 Deploying YAML Manifests Using kapp

Problem

You have installed kapp (see Recipe 6.12), and now you want to deploy and manage your YAML manifests using kapp.

Solution

kapp considers a set of resources with the same label as an application. Suppose you have a folder named *manifests/* that contains the YAML file to deploy an NGINX server. kapp will treat all these manifests as a single application:

```
$ cat manifests/deploy.yaml
apiVersion: apps/v1
kind: Deployment
metadata:
  name: nginx
  labels:
    app: nginx
spec:
  replicas: 1
  selector:
    matchLabels:
      app: nginx
  template:
    metadata:
      labels:
        app: nginx
    spec:
      containers:
      - name: nginx
        image: nginx:1.25.2
        ports:
```

```
            - containerPort: 80
$ cat manifests/svc.yaml
apiVersion:  v1
kind: Service
metadata:
  name: nginx
spec:
  selector:
    app: nginx
  ports:
  - port: 80
```

To deploy these manifests as an application with the label `nginx`, use the following:

```
$ kapp deploy -a nginx -f manifests/
...
Namespace  Name   Kind        Age  Op     Op st.  Wait to     Rs  Ri
default    nginx  Deployment  -    create -       reconcile   -   -
^          nginx  Service     -    create -       reconcile   -   -
...
Continue? [yN]:
```

kapp will provide an overview of the resources that will be created on the cluster and ask for confirmation from the user. To update the application, all you need to do is update the YAML files in the *manifests/* folder and rerun the `deploy` command. You can add the `--diff-changes` option to view a diff of the updated YAML.

Discussion

After deploying applications using kapp, you can manage their lifecycle as well. For example, to inspect the resources created for an app deployment, do this:

```
$ kapp inspect -a nginx
...
Name   Namespaces  Lcs   Lca
nginx  default     true  4s
...
```

To list all the deployed applications, do this:

```
$ kapp ls
...
Name   Namespaces  Lcs   Lca
nginx  default     true  4s
...
```

And to delete an application deployed using kapp, do this:

```
$ kapp delete -a nginx
```

## CHAPTER 7

Exploring the Kubernetes API and Key Metadata

In this chapter, we present recipes that address basic interactions with Kubernetes objects as well as the API. Every object in Kubernetes (*https://oreil.ly/kMcj7*), no matter if namespaced like a deployment or cluster-wide like a node, has certain fields available—for example, metadata, spec, and status. The spec describes the desired state for an object (the specification), and the status captures the actual state of the object, managed by the Kubernetes API server.

7.1 Discovering the Kubernetes API Server's Endpoints

Problem

You want to discover the various API endpoints available on the Kubernetes API server.

Solution

Here we assume you've spun up a development cluster like kind or Minikube locally. You can run kubectl proxy in a separate terminal. The proxy lets you easily access the Kubernetes server API with an HTTP client such as curl, without needing to worry about authentication and certificates. After running kubectl proxy, you should be able to reach the API server on port 8001, as shown here:

```
$ curl http://localhost:8001/api/v1/
{
  "kind": "APIResourceList",
  "groupVersion": "v1",
  "resources": [
```

```
{
  "name": "bindings",
  "singularName": "",
  "namespaced": true,
  "kind": "Binding",
  "verbs": [
    "create"
  ]
},
{
  "name": "componentstatuses",
  "singularName": "",
  "namespaced": false,
  ...
```

This lists all the objects exposed by the Kubernetes API. At the top of the list you can see an example of an object with kind set to Binding as well as the allowed operations on this object (here, create).

Note that another convenient way to discover the API endpoints is to use the kubectl api-resources command.

Discussion

You can discover all the API groups by calling the following endpoint:

```
$ curl http://localhost:8001/apis/
{
  "kind": "APIGroupList",
  "apiVersion": "v1",
  "groups": [
    {
      "name": "apiregistration.k8s.io",
      "versions": [
        {
          "groupVersion": "apiregistration.k8s.io/v1",
          "version": "v1"
        }
      ],
      "preferredVersion": {
        "groupVersion": "apiregistration.k8s.io/v1",
        "version": "v1"
      }
    },
    {
      "name": "apps",
      "versions": [
      ...
```

Pick some API groups to explore from this list, such as the following:

- `/apis/apps`
- `/apis/storage.k8s.io`
- `/apis/flowcontrol.apiserver.k8s.io`
- `/apis/autoscaling`

Each of these endpoints corresponds to an API group. The core API objects are available in the `v1` group at `/api/v1`, whereas other newer API objects are available in named groups under the `/apis/` endpoint, such as `storage.k8s.io/v1` and `apps/v1`. Within a group, API objects are versioned (e.g., `v1`, `v2`, `v1alpha`, `v1beta1`) to indicate the maturity of the objects. Pods, services, config maps, and secrets, for example, are all part of the `/api/v1` API group, whereas the `/apis/autoscaling` group has `v1` and `v2` versions.

The group an object is part of is what is referred to as the `apiVersion` in the object specification, available via the API reference (*https://oreil.ly/fvO82*).

See Also

- Kubernetes API overview (*https://oreil.ly/sANzL*)
- Kubernetes API conventions (*https://oreil.ly/ScJvH*)

7.2 Understanding the Structure of a Kubernetes Manifest

Problem

Although Kubernetes does have convenient generators like `kubectl run` and `kubectl create`, you must to learn how to write Kubernetes manifests to embrace the declarative nature of Kubernetes object specifications. To do this, you need to understand the general structure of manifests.

Solution

In Recipe 7.1, you learned about the various API groups and how to discover which group a particular object is in.

All API resources are either objects or lists. All resources have a `kind` and an `apiVersion`. In addition, every object `kind` must have `metadata`. The `metadata` contains the name of the object, the namespace it is in (see Recipe 7.3), and optionally some labels (see Recipe 7.6) and annotations (see Recipe 7.7).

A pod, for example, will be of kind Pod and apiVersion v1, and the beginning of a simple manifest written in YAML will look like this:

```
apiVersion: v1
kind: Pod
metadata:
  name: mypod
...
```

To complete a manifest, most objects will have a spec and, once created, will also return a status that describes the current state of the object:

```
apiVersion: v1
kind: Pod
metadata:
  name: mypod
spec:
  ...
status:
  ...
```

Discussion

Kubernetes manifests can be used to define the desired state of your cluster. Because manifests are files, they can be stored in a version control system like Git. This allows for distributed and asynchronous collaboration among developers and operators and also enables the creation of automation pipelines for continuous integration and deployment. This is the basic idea behind GitOps, in which any changes to a system are made by changing a source of truth in a version control system. Because all changes are logged in the system, it is possible to revert to previous states or reproduce a given state multiple times. Infrastructure as code (IaC) is a term often used when the declarative source of truth is describing the state of infrastructure (as opposed to applications).

See Also

- Objects in Kubernetes (*https://oreil.ly/EONxU*)

7.3 Creating Namespaces to Avoid Name Collisions

Problem

You want to create two objects with the same name but want to avoid naming collisions.

Solution

Create two namespaces and create one object in each.

If you don't specify anything, objects are created in the default namespace. Try creating a second namespace called my-app, as shown here, and list the existing namespaces. You will see the default namespace, other namespaces that were created on start-up (kube-system, kube-public, and kube-node-lease), and the my-app namespace you just created:

```
$ kubectl create namespace my-app
namespace/my-app created

$ kubectl get ns
NAME               STATUS    AGE
default            Active    5d20h
kube-node-lease    Active    5d20h
kube-public        Active    5d20h
kube-system        Active    5d20h
my-app             Active    13s
```

Alternatively, you can write a manifest to create your namespace. If you save the following manifest as *app.yaml*, you can then create the namespace with the kubectl apply -f app.yaml command:

```
apiVersion: v1
kind: Namespace
metadata:
  name: my-app
```

Discussion

Attempting to start two objects with the same name in the same namespace (e.g., default) leads to a collision, and an error is returned by the Kubernetes API server. However, if you start the second object in a different namespace, the API server will create it:

```
$ kubectl run foobar --image=nginx:latest
pod/foobar created

$ kubectl run foobar --image=nginx:latest
Error from server (AlreadyExists): pods "foobar" already exists

$ kubectl run foobar --image=nginx:latest --namespace my-app
pod/foobar created
```

The kube-system namespace is reserved for administrators, whereas the kube-public namespace (*https://oreil.ly/kQFsq*) is meant to store public objects available to any users of the cluster.

7.4 Setting Quotas Within a Namespace

Problem

You want to limit the resources available in a namespace—for example, the overall number of pods that can run in the namespace.

Solution

Use a `ResourceQuota` object to specify the limitations on a namespace basis.

Start by creating a manifest for a resource quota and saving it in a file called *resource-quota-pods.yaml*:

```
apiVersion: v1
kind: ResourceQuota
metadata:
  name: podquota
spec:
  hard:
    pods: "10"
```

Then create a new namespace and apply the quota to it:

```
$ kubectl create namespace my-app
namespace/my-app created

$ kubectl apply -f resource-quota-pods.yaml --namespace=my-app
resourcequota/podquota created

$ kubectl describe resourcequota podquota --namespace=my-app
Name:       podquota
Namespace:  my-app
Resource    Used  Hard
--------    ----  ----
pods        1     10
```

Discussion

You can set a number of quotas on a per-namespace basis, including but not limited to pods, secrets, and config maps.

See Also

- Configure Quotas for API Objects (*https://oreil.ly/jneBT*)

7.5 Labeling an Object

Problem

You want to label an object so that you can easily find it later. The label can be used for further end-user queries (see Recipe 7.6) or in the context of system automation.

Solution

Use the `kubectl label` command. For example, to label a pod named `foobar` with the key/value pair `tier=frontend`, do this:

```
$ kubectl label pods foobar tier=frontend
pod/foobar labeled
```

 Check the complete help for the command (`kubectl label --help`). You can use it to find out how to remove labels, overwrite existing ones, and even label all resources in a namespace.

Discussion

In Kubernetes, you use labels to organize objects in a flexible, nonhierarchical manner. A label is a key/value pair without any predefined meaning for Kubernetes. In other words, the content of the key/value pair is not interpreted by the system. You can use labels to express membership (e.g., object X belongs to department ABC), environments (e.g., this service runs in production), or really anything you need to organize your objects. There are some common useful labels that you can read about in the Kubernetes documentation (*https://oreil.ly/SMl_N*). Note that labels do have restrictions concerning their length and allowed values (*https://oreil.ly/AzeM8*). However, there is a community guideline (*https://oreil.ly/lTkhW*) for naming keys.

7.6 Using Labels for Queries

Problem

You want to query objects efficiently.

Solution

Use the `kubectl get --selector` command. For example, given the following pods:

```
$ kubectl get pods --show-labels
NAME       READY  STATUS   RESTARTS    AGE    LABELS
foobar     1/1    Running  0           18m    run=foobar,tier=frontend
nginx1     1/1    Running  0           72s    app=nginx,run=nginx1
nginx2     1/1    Running  0           68s    app=nginx,run=nginx2
nginx3     1/1    Running  0           65s    app=nginx,run=nginx3
```

you can select the pods that belong to the NGINX app (`app=nginx`):

```
$ kubectl get pods --selector app=nginx
NAME       READY  STATUS   RESTARTS  AGE
nginx1     1/1    Running  0         3m45s
nginx2     1/1    Running  0         3m41s
nginx3     1/1    Running  0         3m38s
```

Discussion

Labels are part of an object's metadata. Any object in Kubernetes can be labeled. Labels are also used by Kubernetes itself for pod selection by deployments (see Recipe 4.1) and services (see Chapter 5).

Labels can be added manually with the `kubectl label` command (see Recipe 7.5), or you can define labels in an object manifest, like so:

```
apiVersion: v1
kind: Pod
metadata:
  name: foobar
  labels:
    tier: frontend
...
```

Once labels are present, you can list them with `kubectl get`, noting the following:

- `-l` is the short form of `--selector` and will query objects with a specified *key=value* pair.

- `--show-labels` will show all the labels of each object returned.

- `-L` will add a column to the results returned with the value of the specified label.

- Many object kinds support set-based querying, meaning you can state a query in a form like "must be labeled with X and/or Y." For example, `kubectl get pods -l 'env in (production, development)'` would give you pods that are in either the production or development environment.

With two pods running, one with label `run=barfoo` and the other with label `run=foobar`, you would get outputs similar to the following:

```
$ kubectl get pods --show-labels
NAME                          READY    ...    LABELS
barfoo-76081199-h3gwx         1/1      ...    pod-template-hash=76081199,run=barfoo
foobar-1123019601-6x9w1       1/1      ...    pod-template-hash=1123019601,run=foobar

$ kubectl get pods -L run
NAME                          READY    ...    RUN
barfoo-76081199-h3gwx         1/1      ...    barfoo
foobar-1123019601-6x9w1       1/1      ...    foobar

$ kubectl get pods -l run=foobar
NAME                          READY    ...
foobar-1123019601-6x9w1       1/1      ...
```

See Also

- Kubernetes documentation on labels and selectors (*https://oreil.ly/ku1Sc*)

7.7 Annotating a Resource with One Command

Problem

You want to annotate a resource with a generic, nonidentifying key/value pair, possibly using non-human-readable data.

Solution

Use the `kubectl annotate` command:

```
$ kubectl annotate pods foobar \
    description='something that you can use for automation'
pod/foobar annotated
```

Discussion

Annotations tend to be used for added automation of Kubernetes. For example, when you create a deployment with the `kubectl create deployment` command, you will notice that the `change-cause` column in your rollout history (see Recipe 4.6) is empty. As of Kubernetes v1.6.0, to start recording the commands that cause changes to the deployment, you can annotate it with the `kubernetes.io/change-cause` key. Given a deployment `foobar`, you might annotate it with the following:

```
$ kubectl annotate deployment foobar \
    kubernetes.io/change-cause="Reason for creating a new revision"
```

Subsequent changes to the deployment will be recorded.

One of the major differences between annotations and labels is that labels can be used as filtering criteria, whereas annotations cannot. Unless you plan to use your metadata for filtering, then it is generally preferable to use annotations.

## CHAPTER 8

Volumes and Configuration Data

A *volume* in Kubernetes is a directory accessible to all containers running in a pod, with the additional guarantee that the data is preserved across restarts of individual containers.

We can distinguish between a few types of volumes:

- *Node-local* ephemeral volumes, such as `emptyDir`
- Generic *networked* volumes, such as `nfs` or `cephfs`
- *Cloud provider–specific* volumes, such as `AWS EBS` or `AWS EFS`
- *Special-purpose* volumes, such as `secret` or `configMap`

Which volume type you choose depends entirely on your use case. For example, for a temporary scratch space, an `emptyDir` would be fine, but when you need to make sure your data survives node failures, you'll want to look into more resilient alternatives or cloud provider–specific solutions.

8.1 Exchanging Data Between Containers via a Local Volume

Problem

You have two or more containers running in a pod and want to be able to exchange data via filesystem operations.

Solution

Use a local volume of type `emptyDir`.

The starting point is the following pod manifest, *exchangedata.yaml*, which has two containers (c1 and c2) that each mount the local volume xchange into their filesystem, using different mount points:

```yaml
apiVersion: v1
kind: Pod
metadata:
  name: sharevol
spec:
  containers:
  - name: c1
    image: ubuntu:20.04
    command:
      - "bin/bash"
      - "-c"
      - "sleep 10000"
    volumeMounts:
      - name: xchange
        mountPath: "/tmp/xchange"
  - name: c2
    image: ubuntu:20.04
    command:
      - "bin/bash"
      - "-c"
      - "sleep 10000"
    volumeMounts:
      - name: xchange
        mountPath: "/tmp/data"
  volumes:
  - name: xchange
    emptyDir: {}
```

Now you can launch the pod, exec into it, create data from one container, and read it out from the other one:

```
$ kubectl apply -f exchangedata.yaml
pod/sharevol created

$ kubectl exec sharevol -c c1 -i -t -- bash
[root@sharevol /]# mount | grep xchange
/dev/vda1 on /tmp/xchange type ext4 (rw,relatime)
[root@sharevol /]# echo 'some data' > /tmp/xchange/data
[root@sharevol /]# exit

$ kubectl exec sharevol -c c2 -i -t -- bash
[root@sharevol /]# mount | grep /tmp/data
/dev/vda1 on /tmp/data type ext4 (rw,relatime)
[root@sharevol /]# cat /tmp/data/data
some data
[root@sharevol /]# exit
```

Discussion

A local volume is backed by the node on which the pod and its containers are running. If the node goes down or you have to carry out maintenance on it (see Recipe 12.9), then the local volume is gone and all the data is lost.

There are some use cases where local volumes are fine—for example, for some scratch space or when the canonical state is obtained from somewhere else, such as an S3 bucket—but in general you'll want to use a persistent volume or one backed by networked storage (see Recipe 8.4).

See Also

- Kubernetes documentation on volumes (*https://oreil.ly/82P1u*)

8.2 Passing an API Access Key to a Pod Using a Secret

Problem

As an admin, you want to provide your developers with an API access key in a secure way; that is, without sharing it in clear text in your Kubernetes manifests.

Solution

Use a local volume of type `secret` (*https://oreil.ly/bX6ER*).

Let's say you want to give your developers access to an external service that is accessible via the passphrase `open sesame`.

First, create a text file called *passphrase* that holds the passphrase:

```
$ echo -n "open sesame" > ./passphrase
```

Next, create the secret (*https://oreil.ly/cCddB*), using the *passphrase* file:

```
$ kubectl create secret generic pp --from-file=./passphrase
secret/pp created

$ kubectl describe secrets/pp
Name:          pp
Namespace:     default
Labels:        <none>
Annotations:   <none>

Type:   Opaque

Data
====
passphrase:    11 bytes
```

From an admin point of view, you're all set now, and it's time for your developers to consume the secret. So let's switch hats and assume you're a developer and want to use the passphrase from within a pod.

You would consume the secret, for example, by mounting it as a volume into your pod and then reading it out as a normal file. Create and save the following manifest, called *ppconsumer.yaml*:

```
apiVersion: v1
kind: Pod
metadata:
  name: ppconsumer
spec:
  containers:
  - name: shell
    image: busybox:1.36
    command:
      - "sh"
      - "-c"
      - "mount | grep access  && sleep 3600"
    volumeMounts:
      - name: passphrase
        mountPath: "/tmp/access"
        readOnly: true
  volumes:
  - name: passphrase
    secret:
      secretName: pp
```

Now launch the pod and take a look at its logs, where you would expect to see the ppconsumer secret file mounted as */tmp/access/passphrase*:

```
$ kubectl apply -f ppconsumer.yaml
pod/ppconsumer created

$ kubectl logs ppconsumer
tmpfs on /tmp/access type tmpfs (ro,relatime,size=7937656k)
```

To access the passphrase from within the running container, simply read out the *passphrase* file in */tmp/access*, like so:

```
$ kubectl exec ppconsumer -i -t -- sh

/ # cat /tmp/access/passphrase
open sesame
/ # exit
```

Discussion

Secrets exist in the context of a namespace, so you need to take that into account when setting them up and/or consuming them.

You can access a secret from a container running in a pod via one of the following:

- A volume (as shown in the Solution, where the content is stored in a `tmpfs` volume)
- Using the secret as an environment variable (*https://oreil.ly/Edsr5*)

Also, note that the size of a secret is limited to 1 MiB.

 `kubectl create secret` deals with three types of secrets, and depending on your use case, you might want to choose different ones:

- The `docker-registry` type is for use with a Docker registry.
- The `generic` type is what we used in the Solution; it creates a secret from a local file, directory, or literal value (you need to base64-encode it yourself).
- With `tls` you can create, for example, a secure SSL certificate for ingress.

`kubectl describe` doesn't show the content of the secret in plain text. This avoids "over-the-shoulder" password grabs. You can, however, easily decode it manually since it's not encrypted, only base64-encoded:

```
$ kubectl get secret pp -o yaml | \
    grep passphrase | \
    cut -d":" -f 2 | \
    awk '{$1=$1};1' | \
    base64 --decode
open sesame
```

In this command, the first line retrieves a YAML representation of the secret, and the second line with the `grep` pulls out the line `passphrase: b3BlbiBzZXNhbWU=` (note the leading whitespace here). Then, the `cut` extracts the content of the passphrase, and the `awk` command gets rid of the leading whitespace. Finally, the `base64` command turns it into the original data again.

 You have the option to encrypt secrets at rest by using the `--encryption-provider-config` option when launching the kube-apiserver.

See Also

- Kubernetes documentation on secrets (*https://oreil.ly/cCddB*)
- Kubernetes documentation on encrypting confidential data at rest (*https:// oreil.ly/kAmrN*)

8.3 Providing Configuration Data to an Application

Problem

You want to provide configuration data to an application without storing it in the container image or hardcoding it into the pod specification.

Solution

Use a config map. These are first-class Kubernetes resources with which you can provide configuration data to a pod via environment variables or a file.

Let's say you want to create a configuration with the key siseversion and the value 0.9. It's as simple as this:

```
$ kubectl create configmap nginxconfig \
    --from-literal=nginxgreeting="hello from nginx"
configmap/nginxconfig created
```

Now you can use the config map in a deployment—say, in a manifest file with the following contents:

```
apiVersion: v1
kind: Pod
metadata:
  name: nginx
spec:
  containers:
  - name: nginx
    image: nginx:1.25.2
    env:
    - name: NGINX_GREETING
      valueFrom:
        configMapKeyRef:
          name: nginxconfig
          key: nginxgreeting
```

Save this YAML manifest as *nginxpod.yaml* and then use kubectl to create the pod:

```
$ kubectl apply -f nginxpod.yaml
pod/nginx created
```

You can then list the pod's container environment variables with the following command:

```
$ kubectl exec nginx -- printenv
PATH=/usr/local/sbin:/usr/local/bin:/usr/sbin:/usr/bin:/sbin:/bin
HOSTNAME=nginx
NGINX_GREETING=hello from nginx
KUBERNETES_PORT_443_TCP=tcp://10.96.0.1:443
...
```

Discussion

We've just shown how to pass in the configuration as an environment variable. However, you can also mount it into the pod as a file, using a volume.

Suppose you have the following config file, *example.cfg*:

```
debug: true
home: ~/abc
```

You can create a config map that holds the config file, as follows:

```
$ kubectl create configmap configfile --from-file=example.cfg
configmap/configfile created
```

Now you can use the config map just as you would any other volume. The following is the manifest file for a pod named oreilly; it uses the busybox image and just sleeps for 3,600 seconds. In the volumes section, there is a volume named oreilly that uses the config map configfile we just created. This volume is then mounted at the path /oreilly inside the container. Hence, the file will be accessible within the pod:

```
apiVersion: v1
kind: Pod
metadata:
  name: oreilly
spec:
  containers:
  - image: busybox:1.36
    command:
      - sleep
      - "3600"
    volumeMounts:
    - mountPath: /oreilly
      name: oreilly
    name: busybox
  volumes:
  - name: oreilly
    configMap:
      name: configfile
```

After creating the pod, you can verify that the *example.cfg* file is indeed inside it:

```
$ kubectl exec -ti oreilly -- ls -l oreilly
total 0
lrwxrwxrwx   1 root    root    18 Mar 31 09:39 example.cfg -> ..data/example.cfg

$ kubectl exec -ti oreilly -- cat oreilly/example.cfg
debug: true
home: ~/abc
```

For a complete example of how to create a config map from a file, see Recipe 11.7.

See Also

- "Configure a Pod to Use a ConfigMap" (*https://oreil.ly/R1FgU*) in the Kubernetes documentation

8.4 Using a Persistent Volume with Minikube

Problem

You don't want to lose data on a disk your container uses—that is, you want to make sure it survives a restart of the hosting pod.

Solution

Use a persistent volume (PV). In the case of Minikube, you can create a PV of type hostPath and mount it just like a normal volume into the container's filesystem.

First, define the PV hostpathpv in a manifest called *hostpath-pv.yaml*:

```
apiVersion: v1
kind: PersistentVolume
metadata:
  name: hostpathpv
  labels:
    type: local
spec:
  storageClassName: manual
  capacity:
    storage: 1Gi
  accessModes:
  - ReadWriteOnce
  hostPath:
    path: "/tmp/pvdata"
```

Before you can create the PV, however, you need to prepare the directory */tmp/pvdata* on the node—that is, the Minikube instance itself. You can get into the node where the Kubernetes cluster is running using minikube ssh:

```
$ minikube ssh

$ mkdir /tmp/pvdata && \
    echo 'I am content served from a delicious persistent volume' > \
    /tmp/pvdata/index.html

$ cat /tmp/pvdata/index.html
I am content served from a delicious persistent volume

$ exit
```

Now that you've prepared the directory on the node, you can create the PV from the manifest file *hostpath-pv.yaml*:

```
$ kubectl apply -f hostpath-pv.yaml
persistentvolume/hostpathpv created

$ kubectl get pv
NAME         CAPACITY    ACCESSMODES    RECLAIMPOLICY    STATUS       ...   ...   ...
hostpathpv   1Gi         RWO            Retain           Available    ...   ...   ...

$ kubectl describe pv/hostpathpv
Name:            hostpathpv
Labels:          type=local
Annotations:     <none>
Finalizers:      [kubernetes.io/pv-protection]
StorageClass:    manual
Status:          Available
Claim:
Reclaim Policy:  Retain
Access Modes:    RWO
VolumeMode:      Filesystem
Capacity:        1Gi
Node Affinity:   <none>
Message:
Source:
    Type:        HostPath (bare host directory volume)
    Path:        /tmp/pvdata
    HostPathType:
Events:          <none>
```

Up to this point, you would carry out these steps in an admin role. You would define PVs and make them available to developers on the Kubernetes cluster.

Now you're in a position to use the PV in a pod, from a developer's perspective. This is done via a *persistent volume claim* (PVC), so called because, well, you literally claim a PV that fulfills certain characteristics, such as size or storage class.

Create a manifest file called *pvc.yaml* that defines a PVC, asking for 200 MB of space:

```
apiVersion: v1
kind: PersistentVolumeClaim
metadata:
```

```
    name: mypvc
spec:
  storageClassName: manual
  accessModes:
  - ReadWriteOnce
  resources:
    requests:
      storage: 200Mi
```

Next, launch the PVC and verify its state:

```
$ kubectl apply -f pvc.yaml
persistentvolumeclaim/mypvc created

$ kubectl get pv
NAME        CAPACITY  ACCESSMODES  ...  STATUS  CLAIM          STORAGECLASS
hostpathpv  1Gi       RWO          ...  Bound   default/mypvc  manual
```

Note that the status of the PV `hostpathpv` has changed from `Available` to Bound.

Finally, it's time to consume the data from the PV in a container, this time via a deployment that mounts it in the filesystem. So, create a file called *nginx-using-pv.yaml* with the following contents:

```
apiVersion: apps/v1
kind: Deployment
metadata:
  name: nginx-with-pv
spec:
  replicas: 1
  selector:
    matchLabels:
      app: nginx
  template:
    metadata:
      labels:
        app: nginx
    spec:
      containers:
      - name: webserver
        image: nginx:1.25.2
        ports:
        - containerPort: 80
        volumeMounts:
        - mountPath: "/usr/share/nginx/html"
          name: webservercontent
      volumes:
      - name: webservercontent
        persistentVolumeClaim:
          claimName: mypvc
```

And launch the deployment, like so:

```
$ kubectl apply -f nginx-using-pv.yaml
deployment.apps/nginx-with-pv created

$ kubectl get pvc
NAME    STATUS  VOLUME      CAPACITY  ACCESSMODES  STORAGECLASS  AGE
mypvc   Bound   hostpathpv  1Gi       RWO          manual        12m
```

As you can see, the PV is in use via the PVC you created earlier.

To verify that the data actually has arrived, you could now create a service (see Recipe 5.1) along with an `Ingress` object (see Recipe 5.5) and then access it like so:

```
$ curl -k -s https://192.168.99.100/web
I am content served from a delicious persistent volume
```

Well done! You've (as an admin) provisioned a persistent volume and (as a developer) claimed it via a persistent volume claim and used it from a deployment in a pod by mounting it into the container filesystem.

Discussion

In the Solution, we used a persistent volume of type `hostPath`. In a production setting, you would not want to use this but rather ask your cluster administrator nicely to provision a networked volume backed by NFS or an Amazon Elastic Block Store (EBS) volume to make sure your data sticks around and survives single-node failures.

Remember that PVs are cluster-wide resources; that is, they are not namespaced. However, PVCs are namespaced. You can claim PVs from specific namespaces using namespaced PVCs.

See Also

- Kubernetes persistent volumes documentation (*https://oreil.ly/IMCId*)
- "Configure a Pod to Use a PersistentVolume for Storage" (*https://oreil.ly/sNDkp*) in the Kubernetes documentation

8.5 Understanding Data Persistency on Minikube

Problem

You want to use Minikube to deploy a stateful application in Kubernetes. Specifically, you would like to deploy a MySQL database.

Solution

Use a `PersistentVolumeClaim` object (see Recipe 8.4) in your pod definition and/or the template for your database.

First you need to make a request for a specific amount of storage. The following *data.yaml* manifest makes a request for 1 GB of storage:

```
apiVersion: v1
kind: PersistentVolumeClaim
metadata:
  name: data
spec:
  accessModes:
    - ReadWriteOnce
  resources:
    requests:
      storage: 1Gi
```

On Minikube, create this PVC and immediately see how a persistent volume is created to match this claim:

```
$ kubectl apply -f data.yaml
persistentvolumeclaim/data created

$ kubectl get pvc
NAME   STATUS   VOLUME                                    CAPACITY ...  ...  ...
data   Bound    pvc-da58c85c-e29a-11e7-ac0b-080027fcc0e7  1Gi       ...  ...  ...

$ kubectl get pv
NAME                                       CAPACITY  ...  ...  ...  ...  ...
pvc-da58c85c-e29a-11e7-ac0b-080027fcc0e7   1Gi        ...  ...  ...  ...  ...
```

You are now ready to use this claim in your pod. In the `volumes` section of the pod manifest, define a volume by name with a PVC type and a reference to the PVC you just created.

In the `volumeMounts` field, you'll mount this volume at a specific path inside your container. For MySQL, you mount it at `/var/lib/mysql`:

```
apiVersion: v1
kind: Pod
metadata:
  name: db
spec:
  containers:
  - image: mysql:8.1.0
    name: db
    volumeMounts:
    - mountPath: /var/lib/mysql
      name: data
    env:
```

```
      - name: MYSQL_ROOT_PASSWORD
        value: root
  volumes:
  - name: data
    persistentVolumeClaim:
      claimName: data
```

Discussion

Minikube is configured out of the box with a default storage class that defines a default persistent volume provisioner. This means that when a persistent volume claim is created, Kubernetes will dynamically create a matching persistent volume to fill that claim.

This is what happened in the Solution. When you created the persistent volume claim called `data`, Kubernetes automatically created a persistent volume to match that claim. If you look a bit deeper at the default storage class on Minikube, you will see the provisioner type:

```
$ kubectl get storageclass
NAME                 PROVISIONER                 ...
standard (default)   k8s.io/minikube-hostpath    ...

$ kubectl get storageclass standard -o yaml
apiVersion: storage.k8s.io/v1
kind: StorageClass
...
provisioner: k8s.io/minikube-hostpath
reclaimPolicy: Delete
```

This specific storage class is using a storage provisioner that creates persistent volumes of type `hostPath`. You can see this by looking at the manifest of the PV that got created to match the claim you created previously:

```
$ kubectl get pv
NAME                                         CAPACITY   ... CLAIM          ...
pvc-da58c85c-e29a-11e7-ac0b-080027fcc0e7     1Gi        ... default/data   ...

$ kubectl get pv pvc-da58c85c-e29a-11e7-ac0b-080027fcc0e7 -o yaml
apiVersion: v1
kind: PersistentVolume
...
  hostPath:
    path: /tmp/hostpath-provisioner/default/data
    type: ""
...
```

To verify that the host volume created holds the database `data`, you can connect to Minikube and list the files in the directory:

```
$ minikube ssh

$ ls -l /tmp/hostpath-provisioner/default/data
total 99688
...
drwxr-x--- 2 999 docker     4096 Mar 31 11:11  mysql
-rw-r----- 1 999 docker 31457280 Mar 31 11:11  mysql.ibd
lrwxrwxrwx 1 999 docker       27 Mar 31 11:11  mysql.sock -> /var/run/mysqld/...
drwxr-x--- 2 999 docker     4096 Mar 31 11:11  performance_schema
-rw------- 1 999 docker     1680 Mar 31 11:11  private_key.pem
-rw-r--r-- 1 999 docker      452 Mar 31 11:11  public_key.pem
...
```

Indeed, you now have data persistence. If the pod dies (or you delete it), your data will still be available.

In general, storage classes allow the cluster administrator to define the various types of storage they might provide. For the developers, this abstracts the type of storage and lets them use PVCs without having to worry about the storage provider itself.

See Also

- Kubernetes persistent volume claim documentation (*https://oreil.ly/8CRZI*)
- Kubernetes storage class documentation (*https://oreil.ly/32-fw*)

8.6 Storing Encrypted Secrets in Version Control

Problem

You want to store all your Kubernetes manifests in version control and safely share them (even publicly), including secrets.

Solution

Use sealed-secrets (*https://oreil.ly/r-83j*). Sealed-secrets is a Kubernetes controller that decrypts one-way encrypted secrets and creates in-cluster `Secret` objects (see Recipe 8.2).

To get started, install the `v0.23.1` release of the sealed-secrets controller from the release page (*https://oreil.ly/UgMpf*):

```
$ kubectl apply -f https://github.com/bitnami-labs/sealed-secrets/
releases/download/v0.23.1/controller.yaml
```

The result will be that you have a new custom resource and a new pod running in the kube-system namespace:

```
$ kubectl get customresourcedefinitions
NAME                         CREATED AT
sealedsecrets.bitnami.com    2023-01-18T09:23:33Z

$ kubectl get pods -n kube-system  -l name=sealed-secrets-controller
NAME                                          READY   STATUS    RESTARTS   AGE
sealed-secrets-controller-7ff6f47d47-dd76s    1/1     Running   0          2m22s
```

Next, download the corresponding release of the kubeseal binary from the release page (*https://oreil.ly/UgMpf*). This tool will allow you to encrypt your secrets.

For example, on macOS (amd64), do the following:

```
$ wget https://github.com/bitnami-labs/sealed-secrets/releases/download/
v0.23.1/kubeseal-0.23.1-darwin-amd64.tar.gz

$ tar xf kubeseal-0.23.1-darwin-amd64.tar.gz

$ sudo install -m 755 kubeseal /usr/local/bin/kubeseal

$ kubeseal --version
kubeseal version: 0.23.1
```

You are now ready to start using sealed-secrets. First, generate a generic secret manifest:

```
$ kubectl create secret generic oreilly --from-literal=password=root -o json \
    --dry-run=client > secret.json

$ cat secret.json
{
    "kind": "Secret",
    "apiVersion": "v1",
    "metadata": {
        "name": "oreilly",
        "creationTimestamp": null
    },
    "data": {
        "password": "cm9vdA=="
    }
}
```

Then use the kubeseal command to generate the new custom SealedSecret object:

```
$ kubeseal < secret.json > sealedsecret.json

$ cat sealedsecret.json
{
  "kind": "SealedSecret",
  "apiVersion": "bitnami.com/v1alpha1",
  "metadata": {
```

```
        "name": "oreilly",
        "namespace": "default",
        "creationTimestamp": null
    },
    "spec": {
      "template": {
        "metadata": {
          "name": "oreilly",
          "namespace": "default",
          "creationTimestamp": null
        }
      },
      "encryptedData": {
        "password": "AgCyN4kBwl/eLt7aaaCDDNlFDp5s93QaQZZ/mm5BJ6SK1WoKyZ45hz..."
      }
    }
  }
}
```

Create the SealedSecret object using the following:

```
$ kubectl apply -f sealedsecret.json
sealedsecret.bitnami.com/oreilly created
```

You can now store *sealedsecret.json* safely in version control.

Discussion

Once you create the SealedSecret object, the controller will detect it, decrypt it, and generate the corresponding secret.

Your sensitive information is encrypted into a SealedSecret object, which is a custom resource (see Recipe 15.4). The SealedSecret is safe to store under version control and share, even publicly. Once a SealedSecret is created on the Kubernetes API server, only the private key stored in the sealed-secret controller can decrypt it and create the corresponding Secret object (which is only base64-encoded). Nobody else, including the original author, can decrypt the original Secret from the Sealed Secret.

While users cannot decrypt the original Secret from the SealedSecret, they may be able to access the unsealed Secret from the cluster. You should configure RBAC to forbid low-privilege users from reading Secret objects from namespaces that they have restricted access to.

You can list the SealedSecret objects in the current namespace using the following:

```
$ kubectl get sealedsecret
NAME      AGE
oreilly   14s
```

See Also

- The sealed-secrets project on GitHub (*https://oreil.ly/SKVWq*)
- Angus Lees's article "Sealed Secrets: Protecting Your Passwords Before They Reach Kubernetes" (*https://oreil.ly/Ie3nB*)

## CHAPTER 9

Scaling

In Kubernetes, scaling can mean different things to different users. We distinguish between two cases:

Cluster scaling
Sometimes called *cluster elasticity*, this refers to the (automated) process of adding or removing worker nodes based on cluster utilization.

Application-level scaling
Sometimes called *pod scaling*, this refers to the (automated) process of manipulating pod characteristics based on a variety of metrics, from low-level signals such as CPU utilization to higher-level ones, such as HTTP requests served per second, for a given pod.

Two kinds of pod-level scalers exist:

Horizontal pod autoscalers (HPAs)
HPAs automatically increase or decrease the number of pod replicas depending on certain metrics.

Vertical pod autoscalers (VPAs)
VPAs automatically increase or decrease the resource requirements of containers running in a pod.

In this chapter, we first examine cluster elasticity for GKE, AKS, and EKS and then discuss pod scaling with HPAs.

9.1 Scaling a Deployment

Problem

You have a deployment and want to scale it horizontally.

Solution

Use the `kubectl scale` command to scale out a deployment.

Let's reuse the `fancyapp` deployment from Recipe 4.5, with five replicas. If it's not running yet, create it with `kubectl apply -f fancyapp.yaml`.

Now suppose that the load has decreased and you don't need five replicas anymore; three is enough. To scale the deployment down to three replicas, do this:

```
$ kubectl get deploy fancyapp
NAME        READY   UP-TO-DATE   AVAILABLE   AGE
fancyapp    5/5     5            5           59s

$ kubectl scale deployment fancyapp --replicas=3
deployment "fancyapp" scaled

$ kubectl get deploy fancyapp
NAME        READY   UP-TO-DATE   AVAILABLE   AGE
fancyapp    3/3     3            3           81s
```

Rather than manually scaling a deployment, you can automate this process; see Recipe 9.2 for an example.

9.2 Using Horizontal Pod Autoscaling

Problem

You want to automatically increase or decrease the number of pods in a deployment, depending on the load present.

Solution

Use an HPA, as described here.

To use HPAs, the Kubernetes Metrics API must be available. To install the Kubernetes Metrics Server, see Recipe 2.7.

First, create an app—a PHP environment and server—that you can use as the target of the HPA:

```
$ kubectl create deployment appserver --image=registry.k8s.io/hpa-example \
    --port 80
deployment.apps/appserver created
$ kubectl expose deployment appserver --port=80 --target-port=80
$ kubectl set resources deployment appserver -c=hpa-example --requests=cpu=200m
```

Next, create an HPA and define the trigger parameter --cpu-percent=40, which means that the CPU utilization should not exceed 40%:

```
$ kubectl autoscale deployment appserver --cpu-percent=40 --min=1 --max=5
horizontalpodautoscaler.autoscaling/appserver autoscaled

$ kubectl get hpa --watch
NAME        REFERENCE              TARGETS    MINPODS   MAXPODS   REPLICAS   AGE
appserver   Deployment/appserver   1%/40%    1         5         1          2m29s
```

In a second terminal session, keep an eye on the deployment:

```
$ kubectl get deploy appserver --watch
```

Finally, in a third terminal session, launch the load generator:

```
$ kubectl run -i -t loadgen --rm --image=busybox:1.36 --restart=Never -- \
    /bin/sh -c "while sleep 0.01; do wget -q -O- http://appserver; done"
```

Since there are three terminal sessions involved in parallel, an overview of the whole situation is provided in Figure 9-1.

```
✕  kubectl
$ kubectl get hpa --watch
NAME        REFERENCE              TARGETS        MINPODS  MAXPODS  REPLICAS  AGE
appserver   Deployment/appserver   <unknown>/40%  1        5        0         6s
appserver   Deployment/appserver   <unknown>/40%  1        5        1         15s
appserver   Deployment/appserver   115%/40%       1        5        1         60s
appserver   Deployment/appserver   115%/40%       1        5        3         75s
appserver   Deployment/appserver   176%/40%       1        5        3         2m
▯
```

```
✕  kubectl
appserver   1/3   1   1   103s
appserver   1/3   1   1   103s
appserver   1/3   3   1   103s
appserver   2/3   3   2   106s
appserver   3/3   3   3   107s
appserver   3/5   3   3   2m43s
appserver   3/5   3   3   2m43s
appserver   3/5   3   3   2m43s
appserver   3/5   5   3   2m43s
appserver   4/5   5   4   2m46s
appserver   5/5   5   5   2m47s
▯
```

```
✕  kubectl
/bin/sh -c "while sleep 0.01; do wget -q -O- http://appserver; done"
If you don't see a command prompt, try pressing enter.
OK!OK!OK!OK!OK!OK!OK!OK!OK!OK!OK!OK!OK!OK!OK!OK!OK!OK!OK!OK!OK!OK!OK!OK!OK!OK!OK!OK!OK!
K!OK!OK!OK!OK!OK!OK!OK!OK!OK!OK!OK!OK!OK!OK!OK!OK!OK!OK!OK!OK!OK!OK!OK!OK!OK!OK!OK!OK!O
!OK!OK!OK!OK!OK!OK!OK!OK!OK!OK!OK!OK!OK!OK!OK!OK!OK!OK!OK!OK!OK!OK!OK!OK!OK!OK!OK!OK!OK
OK!OK!OK!OK!OK!OK!OK!OK!OK!OK!OK!OK!OK!OK!OK!OK!OK!OK!OK!OK!OK!OK!OK!OK!OK!OK!OK!OK!OK!
K!OK!OK!OK!OK!OK!OK!OK!OK!OK!OK!OK!OK!OK!OK!OK!OK!OK!OK!OK!OK!OK!OK!OK!OK!OK!OK!OK!OK!O
!OK!OK!OK!OK!OK!OK!OK!OK!OK!OK!OK!OK!OK!OK!OK!OK!OK!OK!OK!OK!OK!OK!OK!OK!OK!OK!OK!OK!OK
OK!OK!OK!OK!OK!OK!OK!OK!OK!OK!OK!OK!OK!OK!OK!OK!OK!OK!OK!OK!OK!OK!OK!OK!OK!OK!OK!OK!OK!
K!OK!OK!OK!OK!OK!OK!OK!OK!OK!OK!OK!OK!OK!OK!OK!OK!OK!OK!OK!OK!OK!OK!OK!OK!OK!OK!OK!OK!O
!OK!OK!OK!OK!OK!OK!OK!OK!OK!OK!OK!OK!OK!OK!OK!OK!OK!OK!OK!OK!OK!OK!OK!OK!OK!OK!OK!OK!OK
OK!OK!OK!OK!OK!OK!OK!OK!OK!OK!OK!OK!OK!OK!OK!OK!OK!OK!OK!OK!OK!OK!OK!OK!OK!OK!OK!OK!OK!
K!OK!OK!OK!OK!OK!OK!OK!OK!OK!OK!OK!OK!OK!OK!OK!OK!OK!OK!OK!OK!OK!OK!OK!OK!OK!OK!OK!OK!O
!OK!OK!OK!OK!OK!OK!OK!OK!OK!OK!OK!OK!OK!OK!OK!OK!OK!OK!OK!OK!OK!OK!OK!OK!OK!OK!OK!OK!OK
```

```
✕  kubectl
$ kubectl proxy
Starting to serve on 127.0.0.1:8001
■
```

Figure 9-1. Terminal sessions for setting up an HPA

In Figure 9-2 showing the Kubernetes dashboard, you can see the effect of the HPA on the appserver deployment.

Pods

Name	Images	Labels	Node
● appserver-df98c8594-5mcsh	gcr.io/google_container s/hpa-example	app: appserver pod-template-hash: df9 8c8594	gke-supersizer pool-01e7dbd3
● appserver-df98c8594-8pgpb	gcr.io/google_container s/hpa-example	app: appserver pod-template-hash: df9 8c8594	gke-supersizer pool-01e7dbd3
● appserver-df98c8594-glc79	gcr.io/google_container s/hpa-example	app: appserver pod-template-hash: df9 8c8594	gke-supersizer pool-01e7dbd3
● appserver-df98c8594-qvrzg	gcr.io/google_container s/hpa-example	app: appserver pod-template-hash: df9 8c8594	gke-supersizer pool-01e7dbd3

Figure 9-2. Kubernetes dashboard, showing the effect of an HPA

See Also

- Kubernetes Event-driven Autoscaling (*https://keda.sh*)
- The HPA walkthrough in the Kubernetes documentation (*https://oreil.ly/b6Pwx*)

9.3 Automatically Resizing a Cluster in GKE

Problem

You want the number of nodes in your GKE cluster to automatically grow or shrink, depending on the utilization.

Solution

Use the GKE Cluster Autoscaler. This recipe assumes you've got the `gcloud` command installed and the environment set up (i.e., you've created a project and enabled billing).

Create a cluster with one worker node and cluster autoscaling enabled:

```
$ gcloud container clusters create supersizeme --zone=us-west1-a \
    --machine-type=e2-small --num-nodes=1 \
    --min-nodes=1 --max-nodes=3 --enable-autoscaling
Creating cluster supersizeme in us-west1-a... Cluster is being health-checked
(master is healthy)...done.
```

```
Created [https://container.googleapis.com/v1/projects/k8s-cookbook/zones/
us-west1-a/clusters/supersizeme].
To inspect the contents of your cluster, go to: https://console.cloud.google.com/
kubernetes/workload_/gcloud/us-west1-a/supersizeme?project=k8s-cookbook
kubeconfig entry generated for supersizeme.
NAME         LOCATION    ...  MACHINE_TYPE  NODE_VERSION     NUM_NODES  STATUS
supersizeme  us-west1-a  ...  e2-small      1.26.5-gke.1200  1          RUNNING
```

At this point in time, when looking at the Google Cloud console, you should see
something like what is shown in Figure 9-3.

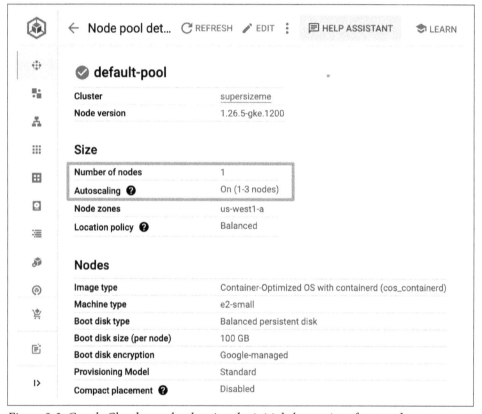

Figure 9-3. Google Cloud console, showing the initial cluster size of one node

Now, launch three pods using a deployment and request cluster resources to trigger
the cluster autoscaling:

```
$ kubectl create deployment gogs --image=gogs/gogs:0.13 --replicas=3
$ kubectl set resources deployment gogs -c=gogs --requests=cpu=200m,memory=256Mi
```

After a while, the deployment will be updated:

```
$ kubectl get deployment gogs
NAME    READY    UP-TO-DATE    AVAILABLE    AGE
gogs    3/3      3             3            2m27s
```

You should now have a cluster of two nodes, as depicted in Figure 9-4.

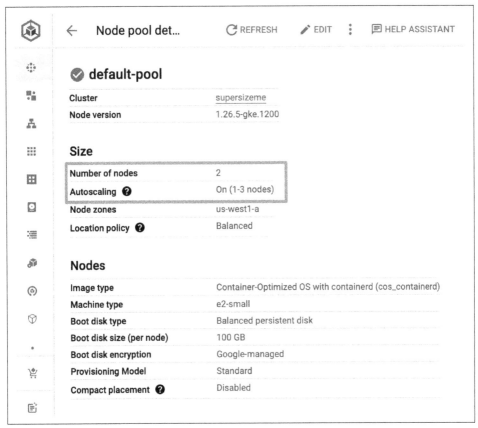

Figure 9-4. Google Cloud console, showing the resulting cluster scaled to two nodes

Discussion

Cluster autoscaling can be enabled or updated on a GKE cluster after it has been created:

```
$ gcloud container clusters update supersizeme --zone=us-west1-a \
    --min-nodes=1 --max-nodes=3 --enable-autoscaling
```

The choice of machine type (*https://oreil.ly/lz7wQ*) used in the cluster nodes is an important factor to consider and depends on the resources required to run your workloads. If your workloads demand more resources, then you should consider using a larger machine type.

Unlike pod scaling, cluster scaling dynamically adds resources to your cluster, which could significantly increase your cloud bill. Ensure that you configure the maximum node count of your GKE cluster appropriately to avoid exceeding your spending limit.

When you don't need the cluster anymore, you should delete it to avoid being charged for unused compute resources:

```
$ gcloud container clusters delete supersizeme
```

See Also

- Cluster Autoscaler (*https://oreil.ly/QHik5*) in the *kubernetes/autoscaler* repo
- Cluster Autoscaler (*https://oreil.ly/g8lfr*) in the GKE docs

9.4 Automatically Resizing an Amazon EKS Cluster

Problem

You want the number of nodes in your AWS EKS cluster to automatically grow or shrink, depending on the utilization.

Solution

Use the Cluster Autoscaler (*https://oreil.ly/6opBo*), a Helm package leveraging AWS autoscaling groups. Follow Recipe 6.1 to install the Helm client that's required to install the package.

First, create a cluster with one worker node and make sure you can access it with kubectl:

```
$ eksctl create cluster --name supersizeme \
    --region eu-central-1 --instance-types t3.small \
    --nodes 1 --nodes-min 1 --nodes-max 3
2023-04-11 12:00:50 [i]  eksctl version 0.136.0-dev+3f5a7c5e0.2023-03-31T10...
2023-04-11 12:00:50 [i]  using region eu-central-1
...
2023-04-11 12:17:31 [i]  kubectl command should work with "/Users/sameersbn/
.kube/config", try 'kubectl get nodes'
2023-04-11 12:17:31 [✔]  EKS cluster "supersizeme" in "eu-central-1" region
is ready

$ aws eks update-kubeconfig --name supersizeme --region eu-central-1
```

Next, deploy the Cluster Autoscaler Helm chart:

```
$ helm repo add autoscaler https://kubernetes.github.io/autoscaler
$ helm install autoscaler autoscaler/cluster-autoscaler \
    --set autoDiscovery.clusterName=supersizeme \
    --set awsRegion=eu-central-1 \
    --set awsAccessKeyID=<YOUR AWS KEY ID> \
    --set awsSecretAccessKey=<YOUR AWS SECRET KEY>
```

At this point, the cluster has only one node:

```
$ kubectl get nodes
NAME                               STATUS   ROLES    AGE   VERSION
ip...eu-central-1.compute.internal Ready    <none>   31m   v1.25.9-eks-0a21954
```

Now, launch five pods using a deployment and request cluster resources to trigger the cluster autoscaling:

```
$ kubectl create deployment gogs --image=gogs/gogs:0.13 --replicas=5
$ kubectl set resources deployment gogs -c=gogs --requests=cpu=200m,memory=512Mi
```

After a while, the deployment will be updated:

```
$ kubectl get deployment gogs
NAME   READY   UP-TO-DATE   AVAILABLE   AGE
gogs   5/5     5            5           2m7s
```

Now your cluster should have scaled up to accommodate the requested resources:

```
$ kubectl get nodes
NAME                               STATUS   ROLES    AGE   VERSION
ip...eu-central-1.compute.internal Ready    <none>   92s   v1.25.9-eks-0a21954
ip...eu-central-1.compute.internal Ready    <none>   93s   v1.25.9-eks-0a21954
ip...eu-central-1.compute.internal Ready    <none>   36m   v1.25.9-eks-0a21954
```

To avoid being charged for unused resources, delete the cluster if you don't need it anymore:

```
$ eksctl delete cluster --name supersizeme --region eu-central-1
```

## CHAPTER 10

Security

Running applications in Kubernetes comes with a shared responsibility between developers and ops folks to ensure that attack vectors are minimized, least-privileges principles are followed, and access to resources is clearly defined. In this chapter, we will present recipes that you can, and should, use to make sure your cluster and apps run securely. The recipes in this chapter cover the following:

- The role and usage of service accounts
- Role-based access control (RBAC)
- Defining a pod's security context

10.1 Providing a Unique Identity for an Application

Problem

You want to grant an application access to restricted resources at a fine-grained level.

Solution

Create a service account with specific secret access and reference it within a pod specification.

To begin, create a dedicated namespace for this and the following recipe called sec:

```
$ kubectl create namespace sec
namespace/sec created
```

Then, create a new service account called myappsa in that namespace and take a closer look at it:

```
$ kubectl create serviceaccount myappsa -n sec
serviceaccount/myappsa created

$ kubectl describe sa myappsa -n sec
Name:                myappsa
Namespace:           sec
Labels:              <none>
Annotations:         <none>
Image pull secrets:  <none>
Mountable secrets:   <none>
Tokens:              <none>
Events:              <none>
```

You can reference this service account in a pod manifest, which we're calling *service-accountpod.yaml*, as shown next. Notice that we are also placing this pod in the sec namespace:

```
apiVersion: v1
kind: Pod
metadata:
  name: myapp
  namespace: sec
spec:
  serviceAccountName: myappsa
  containers:
  - name: main
    image: busybox:1.36
    command:
      - "bin/sh"
      - "-c"
      - "sleep 10000"
```

Create the pod:

```
$ kubectl apply -f serviceaccountpod.yaml
pod/myapp created
```

The service account's API credentials will be automounted at */var/run/secrets/kubernetes.io/serviceaccount/token*:

```
$ kubectl exec myapp -n sec -- \
    cat /var/run/secrets/kubernetes.io/serviceaccount/token
eyJhbGciOiJSUzI1NiIsImtpZCI6IkdHeTRHOUUwWNl ...
```

Indeed, the myappsa service account token has been mounted in the expected place in the pod and can be used going forward.

While a service account on its own is not super useful, it forms the basis for fine-grained access control; see Recipe 10.2 for more on this.

Discussion

Being able to identify an entity is the prerequisite for authentication and authorization. From the API server's point of view, there are two sorts of entities: human users and applications. While user identity (management) is outside of the scope of Kubernetes, there is a first-class resource representing the identity of an app: the service account.

Technically, the authentication of an app is captured by the token available in a file at the location */var/run/secrets/kubernetes.io/serviceaccount/token*, which is mounted automatically through a secret. The service accounts are namespaced resources and are represented as follows:

```
system:serviceaccount:$NAMESPACE:$SERVICEACCOUNT
```

Listing the service accounts in a certain namespace gives you something like the following:

```
$ kubectl get sa -n sec
NAME      SECRETS   AGE
default   0         3m45s
myappsa   0         3m2s
```

Notice the service account called `default` here. This is created automatically; if you don't set the service account for a pod explicitly, as was done in the solution, it will be assigned the `default` service account in its namespace.

See Also

- "Managing Service Accounts" (*https://oreil.ly/FsNK7*) in the Kubernetes documentation
- "Configure Service Accounts for Pods" (*https://oreil.ly/mNP_M*) in the Kubernetes documentation
- "Pull an Image from a Private Registry" (*https://oreil.ly/Fg06V*) in the Kubernetes documentation

10.2 Listing and Viewing Access Control Information

Problem

You want to learn what actions you're allowed to do—for example, updating a deployment or listing secrets.

Solution

The following solution assumes you're using RBAC as the authorization mode (*https://oreil.ly/K7y65*). RBAC is the default mode for access control on Kubernetes.

To check if a certain action on a resource is allowed for a specific user, use `kubectl auth can-i`. For example, you can execute this command to check if the service account called `system:serviceaccount:sec:myappsa` that you created in the previous recipe is allowed to list pods in the namespace `sec`:

```
$ kubectl auth can-i list pods --as=system:serviceaccount:sec:myappsa -n=sec
no
```

You can assign roles to a service account using Kubernetes's built-in RBAC system. For example, you can give the service account permission to view all resources in a given namespace by assigning it the predefined `view` cluster role for that namespace:

```
$ kubectl create rolebinding my-sa-view \
    --clusterrole=view \
    --serviceaccount=sec:myappsa \
    --namespace=sec
rolebinding.rbac.authorization.k8s.io/my-sa-view created
```

Now if you run the same `can-i` command, you'll see that the service account now has permission to read pods in the `sec` namespace:

```
$ kubectl auth can-i list pods --as=system:serviceaccount:sec:myappsa -n=sec
yes
```

> For this recipe to work on Minikube, depending on the version you are running, you may need to add the parameter `--extra-config=apiserver.authorization-mode=Node,RBAC` when starting your Minikube cluster.

To list the roles available in a namespace, do this:

```
$ kubectl get roles -n=kube-system
extension-apiserver-authentication-reader       2023-04-14T15:06:36Z
kube-proxy                                      2023-04-14T15:06:38Z
kubeadm:kubelet-config                          2023-04-14T15:06:36Z
kubeadm:nodes-kubeadm-config                    2023-04-14T15:06:36Z
system::leader-locking-kube-controller-manager  2023-04-14T15:06:36Z
system::leader-locking-kube-scheduler           2023-04-14T15:06:36Z
system:controller:bootstrap-signer              2023-04-14T15:06:36Z
system:controller:cloud-provider                2023-04-14T15:06:36Z
system:controller:token-cleaner                 2023-04-14T15:06:36Z
system:persistent-volume-provisioner            2023-04-14T15:06:39Z

$ kubectl get clusterroles
NAME                                            CREATED AT
```

```
admin                          2023-04-14T15:06:36Z
cluster-admin                  2023-04-14T15:06:36Z
edit                           2023-04-14T15:06:36Z
kubeadm:get-nodes              2023-04-14T15:06:37Z
system:aggregate-to-admin      2023-04-14T15:06:36Z
system:aggregate-to-edit       2023-04-14T15:06:36Z
system:aggregate-to-view       2023-04-14T15:06:36Z
system:auth-delegator          2023-04-14T15:06:36Z
...
```

The output shows the predefined roles, which you can use directly for users and service accounts.

To further explore a certain role and understand what actions are allowed, use the following:

```
$ kubectl describe clusterroles/view
Name:          view
Labels:        kubernetes.io/bootstrapping=rbac-defaults
               rbac.authorization.k8s.io/aggregate-to-edit=true
Annotations:   rbac.authorization.kubernetes.io/autoupdate=true
PolicyRule:
  Resources                             Non-Resource URLs      ...  ...
  ---------                             -----------------      ---  ---
  bindings                              []                     ...  ...
  configmaps                            []                     ...  ...
  cronjobs.batch                        []                     ...  ...
  daemonsets.extensions                 []                     ...  ...
  deployments.apps                      []                     ...  ...
  deployments.extensions                []                     ...  ...
  deployments.apps/scale                []                     ...  ...
  deployments.extensions/scale          []                     ...  ...
  endpoints                             []                     ...  ...
  events                                []                     ...  ...
  horizontalpodautoscalers.autoscaling  []                     ...  ...
  ingresses.extensions                  []                     ...  ...
  jobs.batch                            []                     ...  ...
  limitranges                           []                     ...  ...
  namespaces                            []                     ...  ...
  namespaces/status                     []                     ...  ...
  persistentvolumeclaims                []                     ...  ...
  pods                                  []                     ...  ...
  pods/log                              []                     ...  ...
  pods/status                           []                     ...  ...
  replicasets.extensions                []                     ...  ...
  replicasets.extensions/scale          []                     ...  ...
  ...
```

In addition to the default roles defined in the kube-system namespace, you can define your own; see Recipe 10.3.

Discussion

As you can see in Figure 10-1, there are a couple of moving parts when dealing with RBAC authorization:

- An entity—that is, a group, user, or service account
- A resource, such as a pod, service, or secret
- A role, which defines rules for actions on a resource
- A role binding, which applies a role to an entity

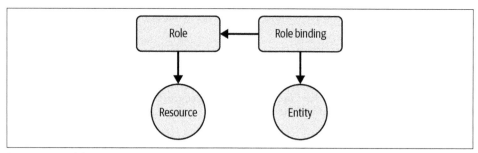

Figure 10-1. The RBAC concept

The actions on a resource that a role uses in its rules are the so-called verbs:

- get, list, watch
- create
- update/patch
- delete

Concerning the roles, we differentiate between two types:

Cluster-wide
Cluster roles and their respective cluster role bindings. Note that you can also attach cluster roles to regular role bindings.

Namespace-wide
Roles and role bindings.

In Recipe 10.3, we will further discuss how you can create your own rules and apply them to users and resources.

See Also

- "Authorization Overview" (*https://oreil.ly/57NdL*) in the Kubernetes documentation

- "Using RBAC Authorization" (*https://oreil.ly/n0i0c*) in the Kubernetes documentation

10.3 Controlling Access to Resources

Problem

For a given user or application, you want to allow or deny a certain action, such as viewing secrets or updating a deployment.

Solution

Let's assume you want to restrict an app to be able to view only pods—that is, list pods and get details about pods.

We'll work in a namespace called `sec`, so start by creating that namespace with `kubectl create namespace sec`.

Then create a pod definition in a YAML manifest, *pod-with-sa.yaml*, using a dedicated service account, `myappsa` (see Recipe 10.1):

```
apiVersion: v1
kind: Pod
metadata:
  name: myapp
  namespace: sec
spec:
  serviceAccountName: myappsa
  containers:
  - name: main
    image: busybox:1.36
    command:
      - "sh"
      - "-c"
      - "sleep 10000"
```

Next, define a role—let's call it `podreader` in the manifest *pod-reader.yaml*—that defines the allowed actions on resources:

```
apiVersion: rbac.authorization.k8s.io/v1
kind: Role
metadata:
  name: podreader
  namespace: sec
rules:
```

```
- apiGroups: [""]
  resources: ["pods"]
  verbs: ["get", "list"]
```

Last but not least, you need to apply the role `podreader` to the service account `myappsa`, using a role binding in *pod-reader-binding.yaml*:

```
apiVersion: rbac.authorization.k8s.io/v1
kind: RoleBinding
metadata:
  name: podreaderbinding
  namespace: sec
roleRef:
  apiGroup: rbac.authorization.k8s.io
  kind: Role
  name: podreader
subjects:
- kind: ServiceAccount
  name: myappsa
  namespace: sec
```

When creating the respective resources, you can use the YAML manifests directly (assuming the service account has already been created):

```
$ kubectl create -f pod-reader.yaml
$ kubectl create -f pod-reader-binding.yaml
$ kubectl create -f pod-with-sa.yaml
```

Rather than creating manifests for the role and the role binding, you can use the following commands:

```
$ kubectl create role podreader \
    --verb=get --verb=list \
    --resource=pods -n=sec

$ kubectl create rolebinding podreaderbinding \
    --role=sec:podreader \
    --serviceaccount=sec:myappsa \
    --namespace=sec
```

Note that this is a case of namespaced access control setup, since you're using roles and role bindings. For cluster-wide access control, you would use the corresponding `create clusterrole` and `create clusterrolebinding` commands.

Discussion

Sometimes it's not obvious whether you should use a role or a cluster role and/or role binding, so here are a few rules of thumb you might find useful:

- If you want to restrict access to a namespaced resource (like a service or pod) in a certain namespace, use a role and a role binding (as we did in this recipe).
- If you want to reuse a role in a couple of namespaces, use a cluster role with a role binding.
- If you want to restrict access to cluster-wide resources such as nodes or to namespaced resources across all namespaces, use a cluster role with a cluster role binding.

See Also

- Kubernetes documentation on using RBAC authorization (*https://oreil.ly/n0i0c*)

10.4 Securing Pods

Problem

You want to define the security context for an app on the pod level. For example, you want to run the app as a nonprivileged process.

Solution

To enforce policies on the pod level in Kubernetes, use the `securityContext` field in a pod specification.

Let's assume you want an app running as a non-root user. For this, you would use the security context on the container level as shown in the following manifest, *securedpod.yaml*:

```
kind: Pod
apiVersion: v1
metadata:
  name: secpod
spec:
  containers:
  - name: shell
    image: ubuntu:20.04
    command:
      - "bin/bash"
      - "-c"
      - "sleep 10000"
    securityContext:
      runAsUser: 5000
```

Now create the pod and check the user under which the container runs:

```
$ kubectl apply -f securedpod.yaml
pod/secpod created

$ kubectl exec secpod -- ps aux
USER        PID %CPU %MEM   VSZ   RSS TTY      STAT START   TIME COMMAND
5000          1  0.0  0.0  2204   784 ?        Ss   15:56   0:00 sleep 10000
5000         13  0.0  0.0  6408  1652 ?        Rs   15:56   0:00 ps aux
```

As expected, it's running as the user with ID 5000. Note that you can also use the
securityContext field on the pod level rather than on specific containers.

Discussion

A more powerful method to enforce policies on the pod level is to use pod security
admission. See "Pod Security Admission" (*https://oreil.ly/ujeV4*) in the Kubernetes
documentation.

See Also

- "Configure a Security Context for a Pod or Container" (*https://oreil.ly/ENH8N*)
  in the Kubernetes documentation

CHAPTER 11
Monitoring and Logging

In this chapter we focus on recipes around monitoring and logging, both on the infrastructure and on the application level. In the context of Kubernetes, different roles typically have different scopes:

Administrator roles

Administrators, such as cluster admins, networking operations folks, or namespace-level admins, focus on the cluster control plane. Example questions they might ask themselves are: Are nodes healthy? Shall we add a worker node? What is the cluster-wide utilization? Are users close to their usage quotas?

Developer roles

Developers mainly think and act in the context of the application or data plane, which may well be—in the age of microservices—a handful to a dozen pods. For example, a person in a developer role might ask: Do I have enough resources allocated to run my app? How many replicas should I scale my app to? Do I have access to the right volumes, and how full are they? Is one of my apps failing and, if so, why?

We will first cover recipes focused on cluster-internal monitoring by leveraging Kubernetes liveness and readiness probes, then focus on monitoring with the Metrics Server (*https://oreil.ly/agm34*) and Prometheus (*https://prometheus.io*), and finally cover logging-related recipes.

11.1 Accessing the Logs of a Container

Problem

You want to access the logs of the application running inside a container that is running in a specific pod.

Solution

Use the kubectl logs command. To see the various options, check the usage, like so:

```
$ kubectl logs --help | more
Print the logs for a container in a pod or specified resource. If the pod has
only one container, the container name is optional.

Examples:
  # Return snapshot logs from pod nginx with only one container
  kubectl logs nginx
...
```

For example, given a pod started by a deployment (see Recipe 4.1), you can check the logs like so:

```
$ kubectl get pods
NAME                             READY   STATUS    RESTARTS   AGE
nginx-with-pv-7d6877b8cf-mjx5m   1/1     Running   0          140m

$ kubectl logs nginx-with-pv-7d6877b8cf-mjx5m
...
2023/03/31 11:03:24 [notice] 1#1: using the "epoll" event method
2023/03/31 11:03:24 [notice] 1#1: nginx/1.23.4
2023/03/31 11:03:24 [notice] 1#1: built by gcc 10.2.1 20210110 (Debian 10.2.1-6)
2023/03/31 11:03:24 [notice] 1#1: OS: Linux 5.15.49-linuxkit
2023/03/31 11:03:24 [notice] 1#1: getrlimit(RLIMIT_NOFILE): 1048576:1048576
2023/03/31 11:03:24 [notice] 1#1: start worker processes
...
```

 If a pod has multiple containers, you can get the logs of any of them by specifying the name of the container using the -c option of kubectl logs.

Discussion

Stern (*https://oreil.ly/o4dxI*) is a useful alternative for viewing pod logs on Kubernetes. It makes it easy to get logs from across namespaces and requires only that you provide a partial pod name in the query (as opposed to using selectors, which can be more cumbersome at times).

11.2 Recovering from a Broken State with a Liveness Probe

Problem

You want to make sure that if the applications running inside some of your pods get into a broken state, Kubernetes restarts the pods automatically.

Solution

Use a liveness probe. If the probe fails, the `kubelet` will restart the pod automatically. The probe is part of the pod specification and is added to the `containers` section. Each container in a pod can have a liveness probe.

A probe can be of three different types: it can be a command that is executed inside the container, an HTTP or gRPC request to a specific route served by an HTTP server inside the container, or a more generic TCP probe.

In the following example, we show a basic HTTP probe:

```
apiVersion: v1
kind: Pod
metadata:
  name: liveness-nginx
spec:
  containers:
  - name: nginx
    image: nginx:1.25.2
    livenessProbe:
      httpGet:
        path: /
        port: 80
```

See Recipe 11.5 for a complete example.

See Also

- Kubernetes container probes documentation (*https://oreil.ly/nrqEP*)

11.3 Controlling Traffic Flow to a Pod Using a Readiness Probe

Problem

Your pods are up and running according to the liveness probes (see Recipe 11.2), but you want to send traffic to them only if the application is ready to serve the requests.

Solution

Add readiness probes (*https://oreil.ly/oU3wa*) to your pod specifications. The following is a straightforward example of running a single pod with the `nginx` container image. The readiness probe makes an HTTP request to port 80:

```
apiVersion: v1
kind: Pod
metadata:
  name: readiness-nginx
spec:
  containers:
  - name: readiness
    image: nginx:1.25.2
    readinessProbe:
      httpGet:
        path: /
        port: 80
```

Discussion

While the readiness probe shown in this recipe is the same as the liveness probe in Recipe 11.2, they typically should be different as the two probes aim to give information about different aspects of the application. The liveness probe checks that the application process is alive, but it may not be ready to accept requests. The readiness probe checks that the application is serving requests properly. As such, only when a readiness probe passes does the pod become part of a service (see Recipe 5.1).

See Also

- Kubernetes container probes documentation (*https://oreil.ly/nrqEP*)

11.4 Protecting Slow-Starting Containers Using a Start-up Probe

Problem

Your pod contains a container that needs additional start-up time on first initialization, but you don't want to use liveness probes (see Recipe 11.2) since this is a requirement only for the first time the pod is launched.

Solution

Add a start-up probe to your pod specification with `failureThreshold` and `period Seconds` set high enough to cover the start-up time for the pod. Similar to liveness probes, start-up probes can be of three types. The following is a straightforward example of running a single pod with the `nginx` container image. The start-up probe makes an HTTP request to port 80:

```
apiVersion: v1
kind: Pod
metadata:
  name: startup-nginx
spec:
  containers:
  - name: startup
    image: nginx:1.25.2
    startupProbe:
      httpGet:
        path: /
        port: 80
      failureThreshold: 30
      periodSeconds: 10
```

Discussion

Sometimes you have to deal with applications that need a long time to start up. For example, an application may need to perform some database migrations that take a long time to complete. In such cases setting up a liveness probe, without compromising the fast response to deadlocks that motivates such a probe, can be tricky. To work around this, in addition to your liveness probe you can set up a start-up probe with the same command, HTTP check, or TCP check, but with a `failureThreshold * periodSeconds` long enough to cover the worse-case start-up time.

If a start-up probe is configured, liveness and readiness probes do not start until it succeeds, making sure those probes don't interfere with the application start-up. This technique can be used to safely implement liveness checks on slow-starting containers, avoiding them getting killed by the `kubelet` before they are up and running.

See Also

- Kubernetes container probes documentation (*https://oreil.ly/nrqEP*)
- "Configure Liveness, Readiness and Startup Probes" (*https://oreil.ly/CoMlg*) in the Kubernetes documentation

11.5 Adding Liveness and Readiness Probes to Your Deployments

Problem

You want to be able to automatically check if your app is healthy and let Kubernetes take action if this is not the case.

Solution

To signal to Kubernetes how your app is doing, add liveness and readiness probes as described here.

The starting point is a deployment manifest, *webserver.yaml*:

```
apiVersion: apps/v1
kind: Deployment
metadata:
  name: webserver
spec:
  replicas: 1
  selector:
    matchLabels:
      app: nginx
  template:
    metadata:
      labels:
        app: nginx
    spec:
      containers:
      - name: nginx
        image: nginx:1.25.2
        ports:
        - containerPort: 80
```

Liveness and readiness probes are defined in the `containers` section of the pod specification. See the introductory examples (Recipes 11.2 and 11.3) and add the following to the container spec in your deployment's pod template:

```
...
        livenessProbe:
          httpGet:
            path: /
            port: 80
          initialDelaySeconds: 2
          periodSeconds: 10
        readinessProbe:
          httpGet:
            path: /
            port: 80
```

```
        initialDelaySeconds: 2
        periodSeconds: 10
...
```

Now you can launch it and check the probes:

```
$ kubectl apply -f webserver.yaml
deployment.apps/webserver created

$ kubectl get pods
NAME                        READY   STATUS    RESTARTS   AGE
webserver-4288715076-dk9c7  1/1     Running   0          2m

$ kubectl describe pod/webserver-4288715076-dk9c7
Name:        webserver-4288715076-dk9c7
Namespace:   default
Priority:    0

...
Status:      Running
IP:          10.32.0.2
...
Containers:
  nginx:
    ...
    Ready:          True
    Restart Count:  0
    Liveness:       http-get http://:80/ delay=2s timeout=1s period=10s #succe...
    Readiness:      http-get http://:80/ delay=2s timeout=1s period=10s #succe...
    ...
...
```

Note that the output of the `kubectl describe` command has been edited down to the important bits; there's much more information available, but it's not pertinent to our problem here.

Discussion

To verify whether a container in a pod is healthy and ready to serve traffic, Kubernetes provides a range of health-checking mechanisms. Health checks, or *probes* as they are called in Kubernetes, are defined on the container level, not on the pod level, and are carried out by two different components:

- The kubelet on each worker node uses the `livenessProbe` directive in the spec to determine when to restart a container. These liveness probes can help overcome ramp-up issues or deadlocks.

- A service load balancing a set of pods uses the `readinessProbe` directive to determine if a pod is ready and hence should receive traffic. If this is not the case, it is excluded from the service's pool of endpoints. Note that a pod is considered ready when all of its containers are ready.

When should you use which probe? That depends on the behavior of the container, really. Use a liveness probe and a `restartPolicy` of either `Always` or `OnFailure` if your container can and should be killed and restarted if the probe fails. If you want to send traffic to a pod only when it's ready, use a readiness probe. Note that in this latter case, the readiness probe can be configured to use the same probing declaration endpoint (e.g., URL) as the liveness probe.

Start-up probes are used to determine if the application in a pod is up and running correctly. They can be used to delay the initialization of liveness and readiness probes, which are likely to fail if the application hasn't correctly started yet.

See Also

- "Configure Liveness, Readiness and Startup Probes" (*https://oreil.ly/CoMlg*) in the Kubernetes documentation

- Kubernetes pod lifecycle documentation (*https://oreil.ly/vEOdP*)

- Kubernetes init containers documentation (*https://oreil.ly/NWpRM*) (stable in v1.6 and above)

11.6 Accessing Kubernetes Metrics in the CLI

Problem

You have installed the Kubernetes Metrics Server (see Recipe 2.7), and you want to access the metrics using the Kubernetes CLI.

Solution

The Kubernetes CLI has the top command that displays the resource usage of nodes and pods:

```
$ kubectl top node
NAME       CPU(cores)   CPU%   MEMORY(bytes)   MEMORY%
minikube   338m         8%     1410Mi          17%


$ kubectl top pods --all-namespaces
NAMESPACE     NAME                              CPU(cores)   MEMORY(bytes)
default       db                                15m          440Mi
default       liveness-nginx                    1m           5Mi
default       nginx-with-pv-7d6877b8cf-mjx5m    0m           3Mi
default       readiness-nginx                   1m           3Mi
default       webserver-f4f7cb455-rhxwt         1m           4Mi
kube-system   coredns-787d4945fb-jrp8j          4m           12Mi
kube-system   etcd-minikube                     48m          52Mi
kube-system   kube-apiserver-minikube           78m          266Mi
...
```

These metrics can also be viewed in a graphical user interface, the Kubernetes dashboard (see Recipe 2.5).

> I can take several minutes for the Metrics Server to become available after having started it. If it is not yet in the ready state, then the top command might produce errors.

11.7 Using Prometheus and Grafana on Minikube

Problem

You want to view and query the system and application metrics of your cluster from a central place.

Solution

Deploy Prometheus and Grafana on Minikube. We'll leverage the kube-prometheus project (*https://oreil.ly/3oyNd*), an independent project that makes it easy to install Prometheus and Grafana on any Kubernetes cluster.

Run the following command to start a new Minikube instance that is correctly configured to run kube-prometheus:

```
$ minikube delete && minikube start --kubernetes-version=v1.27.0 \
    --memory=6g --bootstrapper=kubeadm \
    --extra-config=kubelet.authentication-token-webhook=true \
    --extra-config=kubelet.authorization-mode=Webhook \
    --extra-config=scheduler.bind-address=0.0.0.0 \
    --extra-config=controller-manager.bind-address=0.0.0.0
```

Ensure the metrics-server add-on is disabled on Minikube:

```
$ minikube addons disable metrics-server
```

Clone the kube-prometheus project:

```
$ git clone https://github.com/prometheus-operator/kube-prometheus.git
```

Change into the cloned repository, and then run the following command that will create a dedicated namespace called monitoring and create the necessary custom resource definitions:

```
$ kubectl apply --server-side -f manifests/setup
$ kubectl wait \
    --for condition=Established \
    --all CustomResourceDefinition \
    --namespace=monitoring
$ kubectl apply -f manifests/
```

To open the Prometheus dashboard, you can use a port forward as shown here, or you can use ingress as defined in Recipe 5.5:

```
$ kubectl --namespace monitoring port-forward svc/prometheus-k8s 9090
```

You can then open Prometheus on *localhost:9090* in your browser.

You can do something similar to access the Grafana dashboard:

```
$ kubectl --namespace monitoring port-forward svc/grafana 3000
```

Then open the Grafana dashboard at *localhost:3000* in your browser.

Use the default credentials to log in: username admin and password admin. You can skip changing the password if you're just running this recipe on your local Minikube instance.

There is a built-in dashboard for the Kubernetes API server. To find it, open the URL *http://localhost:3000/dashboards* or navigate to the Dashboards using the left menu bar. Find the dashboard called "Kubernetes / API server"; open it, and you should see a page like the one shown in Figure 11-1.

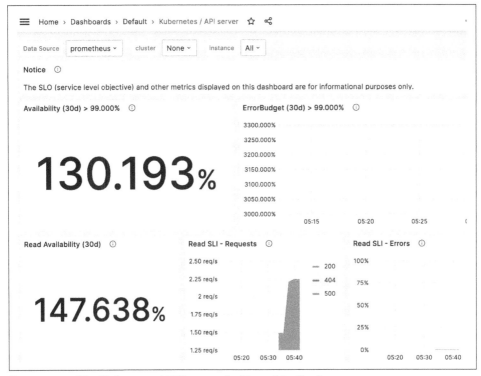

Figure 11-1. The Kubernetes/API server dashboard in Grafana

Discussion

This recipe provides a great way to start experimenting with Grafana and Prometheus and shows how to use an example built-in dashboard to get up and running quickly. Once you start deploying your own custom workloads and applications, you can create your own custom queries and dashboards that will provide metrics that are more specific to your workloads. You can learn more about Prometheus queries in the Prometheus querying reference documentation (*https://oreil.ly/23dQ9*), and more about Grafana dashboards in the Grafana documentation (*https://oreil.ly/nf6jI*).

See Also

- kube-prometheus on GitHub (*https://oreil.ly/3oyNd*)
- Prometheus Operator on GitHub (*https://oreil.ly/q6pdv*)
- Prometheus Operator (*https://prometheus-operator.dev*)
- Prometheus (*https://prometheus.io*)
- Grafana (*https://grafana.com*)

## CHAPTER 12

Maintenance and Troubleshooting

In this chapter, you will find recipes that deal with both app-level and cluster-level maintenance. We cover various aspects of troubleshooting, from debugging pods and containers to testing service connectivity, interpreting a resource's status, and maintaining nodes. Last but not least, we look at how to deal with etcd, the Kubernetes control-plane storage component. This chapter is relevant for both cluster admins and app developers.

12.1 Enabling Autocomplete for kubectl

Problem

It is cumbersome to type full commands and arguments for the kubectl CLI, so you want an autocomplete function for it.

Solution

Enable autocompletion for kubectl.

For the bash shell, you can enable kubectl autocompletion in your current shell with the following command:

```
$ source <(kubectl completion bash)
```

Add this to your ~/.bashrc file so that autocomplete loads in all of your shell sessions:

```
$ echo 'source <(kubectl completion bash)' >>~/.bashrc
```

Note that autocompletion for bash depends on bash-completion (*https://oreil.ly/ AdlLN*) being installed.

For the zsh shell, you can enable `kubectl` autocompletion with the following command:

```
$ source <(kubectl completion zsh)
```

And you can add this same command to your *~/.zshrc* file for autocomplete to load in all your shell sessions.

For autocompletion to work in zsh, you may need to have these commands at the start of your *~/.zshrc* file:

```
autoload -Uz compinit
compinit
```

For other operating systems and shells, please check the documentation (*https://oreil.ly/G3das*).

Discussion

Another popular improvement to the `kubectl` developer experience is to define an alias to shorten `kubectl` to just the letter k. This can be achieved by executing the following commands or adding them to your shell start-up script:

```
alias k=kubectl
complete -o default -F __start_kubectl k
```

Then, you can simply type commands like k `apply -f myobject.yaml`. This combined with autocompletion makes life a lot easier.

See Also

- Overview of `kubectl` (*https://oreil.ly/mu6PZ*)
- `kubectl` Cheat Sheet (*https://oreil.ly/Yrk3C*)

12.2 Removing a Pod from a Service

Problem

You have a well-defined service (see Recipe 5.1) backed by several pods. But one of the pods is causing problems (e.g., crashing or not responding), and you want to take it out of the list of endpoints to examine it at a later time.

Solution

Relabel the pod using the --overwrite option—this will allow you to change the value of the run label on the pod. By overwriting this label, you can ensure that it will not be selected by the service selector (Recipe 5.1) and will be removed from the list of endpoints. At the same time, the replica set watching over your pods will see that a pod has disappeared and will start a new replica.

To see this in action, start with a straightforward deployment generated with kubectl run (see Recipe 4.5):

```
$ kubectl create deployment nginx --image nginx:1.25.2 --replicas 4
```

When you list the pods and show the label with key app, you'll see four pods with the value nginx (app=nginx is the label that is automatically generated by the kubectl create deployment command):

```
$ kubectl get pods -Lapp
NAME                       READY   STATUS    RESTARTS   AGE    APP
nginx-748c667d99-85zxr     1/1     Running   0          14m    nginx
nginx-748c667d99-jrhpc     1/1     Running   0          14m    nginx
nginx-748c667d99-rddww     1/1     Running   0          14m    nginx
nginx-748c667d99-x6h6h     1/1     Running   0          14m    nginx
```

You can then expose this deployment with a service and check the endpoints, which correspond to the IP addresses of each pod:

```
$ kubectl expose deployments nginx --port 80

$ kubectl get endpoints
NAME         ENDPOINTS                                              AGE
kubernetes   192.168.49.2:8443                                      3h36m
nginx        10.244.0.10:80,10.244.0.11:80,10.244.0.13:80 + 1 more... 13m
```

Let's imagine that the first pod in the list is causing problems, even though its status is *Running*.

Moving the first pod out of the service pool via relabeling is done with a single command:

```
$ kubectl label pod nginx-748c667d99-85zxr app=notworking --overwrite
```

> To find the IP address of a pod, you can use a Go template to format the pod information and show only its IP address:
> ```
> $ kubectl get pod nginx-748c667d99-jrhpc \
>     --template '{{.status.podIP}}'
> 10.244.0.11
> ```

You will see a new pod appear with the label `app=nginx`, and you will see that your nonworking pod still exists but no longer appears in the list of service endpoints:

```
$ kubectl get pods -Lapp
NAME                       READY   STATUS    RESTARTS   AGE     APP
nginx-748c667d99-85zxr     1/1     Running   0          14m     notworking
nginx-748c667d99-jrhpc     1/1     Running   0          14m     nginx
nginx-748c667d99-rddww     1/1     Running   0          14m     nginx
nginx-748c667d99-x6h6h     1/1     Running   0          14m     nginx
nginx-748c667d99-xfgqp     1/1     Running   0          2m17s   nginx

$ kubectl describe endpoints nginx
Name:             nginx
Namespace:        default
Labels:           app=nginx
Annotations:      endpoints.kubernetes.io/last-change-trigger-time: 2023-04-13T13...
Subsets:
  Addresses:          10.244.0.10,10.244.0.11,10.244.0.13,10.244.0.9
  NotReadyAddresses:  <none>
  Ports:
    Name      Port  Protocol
    ----      ----  --------
    <unset>   80    TCP

Events:  <none>
```

12.3 Accessing a ClusterIP Service Outside the Cluster

Problem

You have an internal service that is causing you trouble, and you want to test that it is working well locally without exposing the service externally.

Solution

Use a local proxy to the Kubernetes API server with `kubectl proxy`.

Let's assume that you have created a deployment and a service as described in Recipe 12.2. You should see an `nginx` service when you list the services:

```
$ kubectl get svc
NAME    TYPE        CLUSTER-IP      EXTERNAL-IP   PORT(S)   AGE
nginx   ClusterIP   10.108.44.174   <none>        80/TCP    37m
```

This service is not reachable outside the Kubernetes cluster. However, you can run a proxy in a separate terminal and then reach it on *localhost*.

Start by running the proxy in a separate terminal:

```
$ kubectl proxy
Starting to serve on 127.0.0.1:8001
```

You can specify the port that you want the proxy to run on with the
`--port` option.

In your original terminal, you can then use your browser or `curl` to access the
application exposed by your service:

```
$ curl http://localhost:8001/api/v1/namespaces/default/services/nginx/proxy/
<!DOCTYPE html>
<html>
<head>
<title>Welcome to nginx!</title>
...
```

Note the specific path to the service; it contains a `/proxy` part. Without this, you get
the JSON object representing the service.

Note that you can now also access the entire Kubernetes API over
localhost using `curl`.

Discussion

This recipe demonstrates an approach that is suitable for debugging and should not
be used for regular access to services in production. Rather, use the secure Recipe 5.5
for production scenarios.

12.4 Understanding and Parsing Resource Statuses

Problem

You want to watch an object, such as a pod, and react to changes in the object's status.
Sometimes these state changes trigger events in CI/CD pipelines.

Solution

Use kubectl get $KIND/$NAME -o json and parse the JSON output using one of the two methods described here.

If you have the JSON query utility jq installed (*https://oreil.ly/qopuJ*), you can use it to parse the resource status. Let's assume you have a pod called jump. You can do this to find out what Quality of Service (QoS) class (*https://oreil.ly/3CcxH*) the pod is in:

```
$ kubectl run jump --image=nginx
pod/jump created
```

```
$ kubectl get po/jump -o json | jq --raw-output .status.qosClass
BestEffort
```

Note that the --raw-output argument for jq will show the raw value and that .status.qosClass is the expression that matches the respective subfield.

Another status query could be around events or state transitions. For example:

```
$ kubectl get po/jump -o json | jq .status.conditions
[
  {
    "lastProbeTime": null,
    "lastTransitionTime": "2023-04-13T14:00:13Z",
    "status": "True",
    "type": "Initialized"
  },
  {
    "lastProbeTime": null,
    "lastTransitionTime": "2023-04-13T14:00:18Z",
    "status": "True",
    "type": "Ready"
  },
  {
    "lastProbeTime": null,
    "lastTransitionTime": "2023-04-13T14:00:18Z",
    "status": "True",
    "type": "ContainersReady"
  },
  {
    "lastProbeTime": null,
    "lastTransitionTime": "2023-04-13T14:00:13Z",
    "status": "True",
    "type": "PodScheduled"
  }
]
```

Of course, these queries are not limited to pods—you can apply this technique to any resource. For example, you can query the revisions of a deployment:

```
$ kubectl create deployment wordpress --image wordpress:6.3.1
deployment.apps/wordpress created

$ kubectl get deploy/wordpress -o json | jq .metadata.annotations
{
  "deployment.kubernetes.io/revision": "1"
}
```

Or you can list all the endpoints that make up a service:

```
$ kubectl get ep/nginx -o json | jq '.subsets'
[
  {
    "addresses": [
      {
        "ip": "10.244.0.10",
        "nodeName": "minikube",
        "targetRef": {
          "kind": "Pod",
          "name": "nginx-748c667d99-x6h6h",
          "namespace": "default",
          "uid": "a0f3118f-32f5-4a65-8094-8e43979f7cec"
        }
      },
      ...
    ],
    "ports": [
      {
        "port": 80,
        "protocol": "TCP"
      }
    ]
  }
]
```

Now that you've seen jq in action, let's move on to a method that doesn't require external tooling—that is, the built-in feature of using Go templates.

The Go programming language defines templates in a package called text/template that can be used for any kind of text or data transformation, and kubectl has built-in support for it. For example, to list all the container images used in the current namespace, do this:

```
$ kubectl get pods -o go-template \
    --template="{{range .items}}{{range .spec.containers}}{{.image}} \
        {{end}}{{end}}"
fluent/fluentd:v1.16-1   nginx
```

Discussion

You may also want to take a look at JSONPath as an alternative way to parse the JSON produced by kubectl. It provides a syntax that can be considered more readable and easier to reason about. Examples can be found in the Kubernetes documentation (*https://oreil.ly/muOnq*).

See Also

- The jq manual (*https://oreil.ly/Z7rul*)
- jqplay (*https://jqplay.org*) to try out queries without installing jq
- The Go `template` package (*https://oreil.ly/qfQAO*)

12.5 Debugging Pods

Problem

You have a situation where a pod is either not getting to or remaining in the running state as expected or fails altogether after some time.

Solution

To systematically discover and fix the cause of the problem, enter an OODA loop (*https://oreil.ly/alw1o*):

1. *Observe.* What do you see in the container logs? What events have occurred? How is the network connectivity?

2. *Orient.* Formulate a set of plausible hypotheses—stay as open-minded as possible and don't jump to conclusions.

3. *Decide.* Pick one of the hypotheses.

4. *Act.* Test the hypothesis. If it's confirmed, you're done; otherwise, go back to step 1 and continue.

Let's take a look at a concrete example where a pod fails. Create a manifest called *unhappy-pod.yaml* with this content:

```
apiVersion: apps/v1
kind: Deployment
metadata:
  name: unhappy
spec:
  replicas: 1
  selector:
    matchLabels:
```

```
      app: nevermind
  template:
    metadata:
      labels:
        app: nevermind
    spec:
      containers:
      - name: shell
        image: busybox:1.36
        command:
        - "sh"
        - "-c"
        - "echo I will just print something here and then exit"
```

Now when you launch that deployment and look at the pod it creates, you'll see it's
unhappy:

```
$ kubectl apply -f unhappy-pod.yaml
deployment.apps/unhappy created

$ kubectl get pod -l app=nevermind
NAME                        READY   STATUS            RESTARTS       AGE
unhappy-576954b454-xtb2g    0/1     CrashLoopBackOff  2 (21s ago)    42s

$ kubectl describe pod -l app=nevermind
Name:             unhappy-576954b454-xtb2g
Namespace:        default
Priority:         0
Service Account:  default
Node:             minikube/192.168.49.2
Start Time:       Thu, 13 Apr 2023 22:31:28 +0200
Labels:           app=nevermind
                  pod-template-hash=576954b454
Annotations:      <none>
Status:           Running
IP:               10.244.0.16
IPs:
  IP:             10.244.0.16
Controlled By:    ReplicaSet/unhappy-576954b454
...
Conditions:
  Type             Status
  Initialized      True
  Ready            False
  ContainersReady  False
  PodScheduled     True
Volumes:
  kube-api-access-bff5c:
    Type:                   Projected (a volume that contains injected data...)
    TokenExpirationSeconds: 3607
    ConfigMapName:          kube-root-ca.crt
    ConfigMapOptional:      <nil>
    DownwardAPI:            true
```

```
QoS Class:                   BestEffort
Node-Selectors:              <none>
Tolerations:                 node.kubernetes.io/not-ready:NoExecute op=Exist...
                             node.kubernetes.io/unreachable:NoExecute op=Exist...
Events:
  Type     Reason     ...   Message
  ----     ------     ---   -------
  Normal   Scheduled  ...   Successfully assigned default/unhappy-576954b454-x...
  Normal   Pulled     ...   Successfully pulled image "busybox" in 2.945704376...
  Normal   Pulled     ...   Successfully pulled image "busybox" in 1.075044917...
  Normal   Pulled     ...   Successfully pulled image "busybox" in 1.119703875...
  Normal   Pulling    ...   Pulling image "busybox"
  Normal   Created    ...   Created container shell
  Normal   Started    ...   Started container shell
  Normal   Pulled     ...   Successfully pulled image "busybox" in 1.055005126...
  Warning  BackOff    ...   Back-off restarting failed container shell in pod...
```

As you can see at the bottom of the description, in the Events section, Kubernetes considers this pod as not ready to serve traffic because "Back-off restarting failed...."

Another way to observe this is by using the Kubernetes dashboard to view the deployment (Figure 12-1), as well as the supervised replica set and the pod (Figure 12-2). With Minikube you can easily open the dashboard by running the command minikube dashboard.

Deployments			
Name	Images	Labels	Pods
unhappy	busybox	-	1 / 1
Back-off restarting failed container shell in pod unhappy-576954b454-xtb2g_default(0424931c-ed29-4be3-b24a-e37f51fc4723)			
wordpress	wordpress	app: wordpress	1 / 1
nginx	nginx	app: nginx	4 / 4
es	docker.elastic.co/elasticsearch/elasticsearch:8.7.0	-	1 / 1
kibana	docker.elastic.co/kibana/kibana:8.7.0	-	1 / 1

Figure 12-1. Deployment in error state

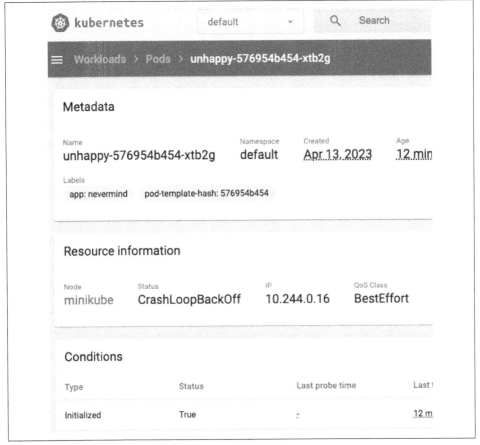

Figure 12-2. Pod in error state

Discussion

An issue, be it a pod failing or a node behaving strangely, can have many different causes. Here are some things you'll want to check before suspecting software bugs:

- Is the manifest correct? Check with a tool such as Kubeconform (*https://oreil.ly/ q_e39*).
- Are you able to run the container locally outside of Kubernetes?
- Can Kubernetes reach the container registry and actually pull the container image?
- Can the nodes talk to each other?
- Can the nodes reach the control plane?
- Is DNS available in the cluster?

- Are there sufficient resources available on the nodes, such as CPU, memory, and disk space?
- Did you restrict the container or the namespace's resource usage?
- What are the events in the object description saying?

See Also

- "Debug Pods" (*https://oreil.ly/nuThZ*) in the Kubernetes documentation
- "Debug Running Pods" (*https://oreil.ly/61xce*) in the Kubernetes documentation
- "Debug Services" (*https://oreil.ly/XrF29*) in the Kubernetes documentation
- "Troubleshooting Clusters" (*https://oreil.ly/LD9oN*) in the Kubernetes documentation

12.6 Influencing a Pod's Start-up Behavior

Problem

For your pod to function properly, it depends on some other service being available. You want to influence the pod's start-up behavior so that it starts only once the pods it depends on are available.

Solution

Use init containers (*https://oreil.ly/NWpRM*) to influence the start-up behavior of a pod.

Imagine you want to launch an NGINX web server that depends on a backend service to serve content. You therefore want to make sure that the NGINX pod starts up only once the backend service is up and running.

First, create the backend service the web server depends on:

```
$ kubectl create deployment backend --image=gcr.io/google-samples/hello-app:2.0
deployment.apps/backend created
$ kubectl expose deployment backend --port=80 --target-port=8080
```

Then you can use the following manifest, *nginx-init-container.yaml*, to launch the NGINX instance and make sure it starts up only when the backend deployment is ready to accept connections:

```
kind: Deployment
apiVersion: apps/v1
metadata:
  name: nginx
spec:
```

```
      replicas: 1
      selector:
        matchLabels:
          app: nginx
      template:
        metadata:
          labels:
            app: nginx
        spec:
          containers:
          - name: webserver
            image: nginx:1.25.2
            ports:
            - containerPort: 80
          initContainers:
          - name: checkbackend
            image: busybox:1.36
            command: ['sh', '-c', 'until nc -w 5 backend.default.svc.cluster.local
                    80; do echo
                    "Waiting for backend to accept connections"; sleep 3; done; echo
                    "Backend is up, ready to launch web server"']
```

Now you can launch the `nginx` deployment and verify whether the init container has done its job by looking at the logs of the pod it is supervising:

```
$ kubectl apply -f nginx-init-container.yaml
deployment.apps/nginx created

$ kubectl get po
NAME                          READY   STATUS    RESTARTS   AGE
backend-8485c64ccb-99jdh      1/1     Running   0          4m33s
nginx-779d9fcdf6-2ntpn        1/1     Running   0          32s

$ kubectl logs nginx-779d9fcdf6-2ntpn -c checkbackend
Server:    10.96.0.10
Address:   10.96.0.10:53


Name: backend.default.svc.cluster.local
Address: 10.101.119.67

Backend is up, ready to launch web server
```

As you can see, the command in the init container indeed worked as planned.

Discussion

Init containers are useful to prevent your application from crash looping while it is waiting for a service to become available. For example, if you are deploying an application that needs to connect to a database server, you can configure an init container that checks and waits for the database server to become ready before your application attempts a connection with it.

However, it is important to keep in mind that Kubernetes can technically kill a pod at any time, even after it was started successfully. Therefore, it is also important that you build resiliency into your application such that it can survive failures in other dependent services.

12.7 Getting a Detailed Snapshot of the Cluster State

Problem

You want to get a detailed snapshot of the overall cluster state for orientation, auditing, or troubleshooting purposes.

Solution

Use the `kubectl cluster-info dump` command. For example, to create a dump of the cluster state in a subdirectory *cluster-state-2023-04-13*, do this:

```
$ mkdir cluster-state-2023-04-13

$ kubectl cluster-info dump --all-namespaces \
    --output-directory=cluster-state-2023-04-13
Cluster info dumped to cluster-state-2023-04-13

$ tree ./cluster-state-2023-04-13
./cluster-state-2023-04-13
├── default
│   ├── daemonsets.json
│   ├── deployments.json
│   ├── es-598664765b-tpw59
│   │   └── logs.txt
│   ├── events.json
│   ├── fluentd-vw7d9
│   │   └── logs.txt
│   ├── jump
│   │   └── logs.txt
│   ├── kibana-5847789b45-bm6tn
│   │   └── logs.txt
    ...
├── ingress-nginx
│   ├── daemonsets.json
│   ├── deployments.json
│   ├── events.json
│   ├── ingress-nginx-admission-create-7qdjp
│   │   └── logs.txt
│   ├── ingress-nginx-admission-patch-cv6c6
│   │   └── logs.txt
```

```
│   ├── ingress-nginx-controller-77669ff58-rqdlq
│   │   └── logs.txt
│   ├── pods.json
│   ├── replicasets.json
│   ├── replication-controllers.json
│   └── services.json
├── kube-node-lease
│   ├── daemonsets.json
│   ├── deployments.json
│   ├── events.json
│   ├── pods.json
│   ├── replicasets.json
│   ├── replication-controllers.json
│   └── services.json
├── kube-public
│   ├── daemonsets.json
│   ├── deployments.json
│   ├── events.json
│   ├── pods.json
│   ├── replicasets.json
│   ├── replication-controllers.json
│   └── services.json
├── kube-system
│   ├── coredns-787d4945fb-9k8pn
│   │   └── logs.txt
│   ├── daemonsets.json
│   ├── deployments.json
│   ├── etcd-minikube
│   │   └── logs.txt
│   ├── events.json
│   ├── kube-apiserver-minikube
│   │   └── logs.txt
│   ├── kube-controller-manager-minikube
│   │   └── logs.txt
│   ├── kube-proxy-x6zdw
│   │   └── logs.txt
│   ├── kube-scheduler-minikube
│   │   └── logs.txt
│   ├── pods.json
│   ├── replicasets.json
│   ├── replication-controllers.json
│   ├── services.json
│   └── storage-provisioner
│       └── logs.txt
├── kubernetes-dashboard
│   ├── daemonsets.json
│   ├── dashboard-metrics-scraper-5c6664855-sztn5
│   │   └── logs.txt
│   ├── deployments.json
│   ├── events.json
│   ├── kubernetes-dashboard-55c4cbbc7c-ntjwk
│   │   └── logs.txt
```

```
|   ├── pods.json
|   ├── replicasets.json
|   ├── replication-controllers.json
|   └── services.json
└── nodes.json

30 directories, 66 files
```

12.8 Adding Kubernetes Worker Nodes

Problem

You need to add a worker node to your Kubernetes cluster, for instance because you want to increase the capacity of your cluster.

Solution

Provision a new machine in whatever way your environment requires (for example, in a bare-metal environment you might need to physically install a new server in a rack, in a public cloud setting you need to create a new VM, etc.), and then install, as daemons, the three components that make up a Kubernetes worker node:

kubelet

> This is the node manager and supervisor for all pods, no matter if they're controlled by the API server or running locally, such as static pods. Note that the kubelet is the final arbiter of what pods can or cannot run on a given node, and it takes care of the following:

> - Reporting node and pod statuses to the API server
> - Periodically executing liveness probes
> - Mounting the pod volumes and downloading secrets
> - Controlling the container runtime (see the following)

Container runtime

> This is responsible for downloading container images and running containers. Kubernetes requires the use of a runtime that conforms to the Container Runtime Interface (CRI) (*https://oreil.ly/6hmkR*), like cri-o (*http://cri-o.io*), Docker Engine (*https://docs.docker.com/engine*), or containerd (*https://containerd.io*).

kube-proxy

> This process dynamically configures iptables rules on the node to enable the Kubernetes service abstraction (redirecting the VIP to the endpoints, one or more pods representing the service).

The actual installation of the components depends heavily on your environment and the installation method used (cloud, kubeadm, etc.). For a list of available options, see the kubelet reference (*https://oreil.ly/8XBRS*) and kube-proxy reference (*https://oreil.ly/mED8e*).

Discussion

Worker nodes, unlike other Kubernetes resources such as deployments or services, are not directly created by the Kubernetes control plane but only managed by it. That means when Kubernetes creates a node, it actually only creates an object that *represents* the worker node. It validates the node by health checks based on the node's metadata.name field, and if the node is valid—that is, all necessary components are running—it is considered part of the cluster; otherwise, it will be ignored for any cluster activity until it becomes valid.

See Also

- "Nodes" (*https://oreil.ly/MQ4ZV*) in the Kubernetes cluster architecture concepts
- "Communication Between Nodes and the Control Plane" (*https://oreil.ly/ePukq*) in the Kubernetes documentation
- "Create Static Pods" (*https://oreil.ly/_OKBq*) in the Kubernetes documentation

12.9 Draining Kubernetes Nodes for Maintenance

Problem

You need to carry out maintenance on a node—for example, to apply a security patch or upgrade the operating system.

Solution

Use the kubectl drain command. For example, list nodes with kubectl get nodes, and then to do maintenance on node 123-worker, do this:

```
$ kubectl drain 123-worker
```

When you are ready to put the node back into service, use kubectl uncordon 123-worker, which will make the node schedulable again.

Discussion

The kubectl drain command first marks the specified node as unschedulable to prevent new pods from arriving (essentially a kubectl cordon). Then it evicts the pods if the API server supports eviction (*https://oreil.ly/xXLII*). Otherwise, it will use `kubectl delete` to delete the pods. The Kubernetes docs have a concise sequence diagram of the steps, reproduced in Figure 12-3.

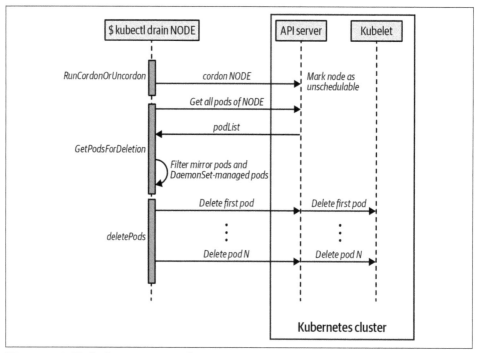

Figure 12-3. Node drain sequence diagram

The `kubectl drain` command evicts or deletes all pods except mirror pods (which cannot be deleted through the API server). For pods supervised by a `DaemonSet`, drain will not proceed without using `--ignore-daemonsets`, and regardless it will not delete any `DaemonSet`-managed pods—those pods would be immediately replaced by the `DaemonSet` controller, which ignores unschedulable markings.

> `drain` waits for graceful termination, so you should not operate on this node until the `kubectl drain` command has completed. Note that `kubectl drain $NODE --force` will also evict pods not managed by a `ReplicationController`, `ReplicaSet`, `Job`, `DaemonSet`, or `StatefulSet`.

See Also

- "Safely Drain a Node" (*https://oreil.ly/upbMl*) in the Kubernetes documentation
- `kubectl drain` reference docs (*https://oreil.ly/YP6zg*)

## CHAPTER 13

Service Meshes

This chapter focuses on one of the building blocks that make it easier to develop distributed, microservices-based applications on Kubernetes: the service mesh. Service meshes like Istio and Linkerd can perform duties such as monitoring, service discovery, traffic control, and security, to name a few. By offloading these responsibilities to the mesh, application developers can focus on delivering added value rather than reinventing the wheel by solving transversal infrastructure concerns.

One of the major benefits of service meshes is that they can apply policies to services transparently, without the services (client and server) needing to know they are part of a service mesh.

In this chapter, we'll run through basic examples using both Istio and Linkerd. For each service mesh, we'll show how you can quickly get up and running using Minikube and implement service-to-service communication inside the mesh while using simple but illustrative service mesh policies. In both examples, we'll deploy a service based on NGINX, and our client invoking the service will be a curl pod. Both will be added to the mesh and the interactions between the services will be governed by the mesh.

13.1 Installing the Istio Service Mesh

Problem

Your organization is using or plans to use a microservices architecture, and you want to lighten the load on developers by offloading the need to build security, service discovery, telemetry, deployment strategies, and other nonfunctional concerns.

Solution

Install Istio on Minikube. Istio is the most widely adopted service mesh and can offload many responsibilities from microservice developers, while also providing operators with centralized governance over security and operations.

First, you'll need to start Minikube with enough resources to run Istio. The exact resource requirements depend on your platform, and you may need to adjust the resource allocations. We have gotten it to work with just under 8 GB of memory and four CPUs:

```
$ minikube start --memory=7851 --cpus=4
```

You can use a Minikube tunnel as a load balancer for Istio. To start it, run this command in a new terminal (it will lock the terminal to show output information):

```
$ minikube tunnel
```

Download and extract the latest version of Istio with the following command (Linux and macOS):

```
$ curl -L https://istio.io/downloadIstio | sh -
```

For Windows, you can install with choco or just extract the *.exe* from the downloadable archive. For more info on downloading Istio, head to Istio's Getting Started guide (*https://oreil.ly/5uFlk*).

Change to the Istio directory. You may need to adapt the directory name depending on the version of Istio that you installed:

```
$ cd istio-1.18.0
```

The istioctl command-line tool is designed to help debug and diagnose your service mesh, and you'll use it to check your Istio configuration in other recipes. It lives in the *bin* directory, so add it to your path like so:

```
$ export PATH=$PWD/bin:$PATH
```

Now you can install Istio. The following YAML file contains an example demo configuration. It intentionally deactivates the use of Istio as an ingress or egress gateway, as we won't be using Istio for ingress here. Store this config in a file called *istio-demo-config.yaml*:

```
apiVersion: install.istio.io/v1alpha1
kind: IstioOperator
spec:
  profile: demo
  components:
    ingressGateways:
    - name: istio-ingressgateway
      enabled: false
    egressGateways:
```

```
    - name: istio-egressgateway
      enabled: false
```

Now use `istioctl` to apply this configuration to Minikube:

```
$ istioctl install -f istio-demo-config.yaml -y
✔ Istio core installed
✔ Istiod installed
✔ Installation complete
```

Finally, make sure Istio is configured to automatically inject Envoy sidecar proxies to services that you deploy. You can enable this for the default namespace with the following command:

```
$ kubectl label namespace default istio-injection=enabled
namespace/default labeled
```

Discussion

This guide makes use of default (which sometimes implies latest) versions of underlying projects like Kubernetes and Istio.

You can customize these versions to match the versions of your current production environment, for instance. To set the version of Istio you want to use, use the `ISTIO_VERSION` and `TARGET_ARCH` parameters when downloading Istio. For example:

```
$ curl -L https://istio.io/downloadIstio | ISTIO_VERSION=1.18.0 \
    TARGET_ARCH=x86_64 sh -
```

See Also

- The official Istio Getting Started guide (*https://oreil.ly/AKCYs*)

13.2 Deploying a Microservice with an Istio Sidecar

Problem

You want to deploy a new service into the service mesh, implying that a sidecar should be automatically injected into the service's pod. The sidecar will intercept all of the service's incoming and outgoing traffic and allow the implementation of routing, security, and monitoring policies (among others) without modifying the implementation of the service itself.

Solution

We'll use NGINX as a simple service to work with. Start by creating a deployment for NGINX:

```
$ kubectl create deployment nginx --image nginx:1.25.2
deployment.apps/nginx created
```

Then expose this as a Kubernetes service:

```
$ kubectl expose deploy/nginx --port 80
service/nginx exposed
```

 Istio does not create new DNS entries on Kubernetes but instead relies on existing services registered by Kubernetes or any other service registry you might be using. Later in the chapter, you'll deploy a `curl` pod that invokes the `nginx` service and set the `curl` host to `nginx` for DNS resolution, but then Istio will work its magic by intercepting the request and allowing you to define additional traffic control policies.

Now list the pods in the default namespace. You should have two containers in the service's pod:

```
$ kubectl get po
NAME                        READY   STATUS    RESTARTS   AGE
nginx-77b4fdf86c-kzqvt      2/2     Running   0          27s
```

If you investigate the details of this pod, you'll find that the Istio sidecar container (based on the Envoy proxy) was injected into the pod:

```
$ kubectl get pods -l app=nginx -o yaml
apiVersion: v1
items:
- apiVersion: v1
  kind: Pod
  metadata:
    labels:
      app: nginx
      ...
  spec:
    containers:
    - image: nginx:1.25.2
      imagePullPolicy: IfNotPresent
      name: nginx
      resources: {}

    ...
kind: List
metadata:
  resourceVersion: ""
```

Discussion

This recipe assumes you have enabled automatic sidecar injection in the namespace using the namespace labeling technique, as shown in Recipe 13.1. However, you might not necessarily want to inject sidecars into every single pod in the namespace. In that case, you can manually choose which pods should include the sidecar and thereby be added to the mesh. You can learn more about manual sidecar injection in the official Istio documentation (*https://oreil.ly/VbHz_*).

See Also

- More information about how to install and configure the sidecar (*https://oreil.ly/E-omC*)
- More information about the role of sidecars in Istio (*https://oreil.ly/TperP*)

13.3 Routing Traffic Using an Istio Virtual Service

Problem

You want to deploy another service onto the cluster that will invoke the nginx service you deployed earlier, but you don't want to write any routing or security logic into the services themselves. You also want to decouple the client and server as much as possible.

Solution

We'll simulate interservice communication within the service mesh by deploying a curl pod that will be added to the mesh and invoke the nginx service.

To decouple the curl pod from the specific pod running nginx, you'll create an Istio virtual service. The curl pod only needs to know about the virtual service. Istio and its sidecars will intercept and route the traffic from the client to the service.

Create the following virtual service specification in a file called *virtualservice.yaml*:

```
apiVersion: networking.istio.io/v1alpha3
kind: VirtualService
metadata:
  name: nginx-vs
spec:
  hosts:
  - nginx
  http:
  - route:
    - destination:
        host: nginx
```

Create the virtual service:

```
$ kubectl apply -f virtualservice.yaml
```

Then run a `curl` pod that you'll use to invoke the service. Because you've deployed the `curl` pod in the `default` namespace and you've activated automatic sidecar injection in this namespace (Recipe 13.1), the `curl` pod will automatically get a sidecar and be added to the mesh:

```
$ kubectl run mycurlpod --image=curlimages/curl -i --tty -- sh
```

If you accidentally exit the `curl` pod's shell, you can always enter the pod again with the kubectl exec command:

```
$ kubectl exec -i --tty mycurlpod -- sh
```

Now you can invoke the `nginx` virtual service from the `curl` pod:

```
$ curl -v nginx
*   Trying 10.152.183.90:80...
* Connected to nginx (10.152.183.90) port 80 (#0)
> GET / HTTP/1.1
> Host: nginx
> User-Agent: curl/8.1.2
> Accept: */*
>
> HTTP/1.1 200 OK
> server: envoy
...
```

You'll see the response from the `nginx` service, but notice how the HTTP header `server: envoy` indicates that the response is actually coming from the Istio sidecar running in the `nginx` pod.

To reference virtual services from `curl`, we're using short names that reference the names of the Kubernetes services (`nginx` in this example). Under the hood, these names are translated into fully qualified domain names, like `nginx.default.svc.cluster.local`. As you can see, the fully qualified name includes a namespace name (`default` in this case). To be safe, for production use cases it is recommend you explicitly use fully qualified names to avoid misconfigurations.

Discussion

This recipe focused on interservice communication within a service mesh (also known as *east–west communication*), which is the sweet spot for this technology.

However, Istio and other services meshes are also able to perform gateway duties (also known as *ingress* and *north–south communication*), such as interactions between clients running outside the mesh (or the Kubernetes cluster) and services running in the mesh.

At the time of writing, Istio's gateway resource is being gradually phased out in favor of the new Kubernetes Gateway API (*https://gateway-api.sigs.k8s.io*).

See Also

- Official reference documentation for Istio virtual services (*https://oreil.ly/Lth6l*).
- Read more about how the Kubernetes Gateway API is expected to replace Istio's Gateway (*https://oreil.ly/6vHQv*).

13.4 Rewriting a URL Using an Istio Virtual Service

Problem

A legacy client is using a URL and path for a service that is no longer valid. You want to rewrite the path dynamically so that the service is correctly invoked, without having to make changes to the client.

You can simulate this problem from your `curl` pod by invoking the path */legacypath* like so, which produces a 404 Not Found response:

```
$ curl -v nginx/legacypath
*   Trying 10.152.183.90:80...
* Connected to nginx (10.152.183.90) port 80 (#0)
> GET /legacypath HTTP/1.1
> Host: nginx
> User-Agent: curl/8.1.2
> Accept: */*
>
< HTTP/1.1 404 Not Found
< server: envoy
< date: Mon, 26 Jun 2023 09:37:43 GMT
< content-type: text/html
< content-length: 153
< x-envoy-upstream-service-time: 20
<
<html>
<head><title>404 Not Found</title></head>
<body>
<center><h1>404 Not Found</h1></center>
<hr><center>nginx/1.25.1</center>
</body>
</html>
```

Solution

Use Istio to rewrite the legacy path so that it reaches a valid endpoint on the service, which in our example will be the root of the `nginx` service.

Update the virtual service to include an HTTP rewrite:

```
apiVersion: networking.istio.io/v1alpha3
kind: VirtualService
metadata:
  name: nginx-vs
spec:
  hosts:
  - nginx
  http:
  - match:
    - uri:
        prefix: /legacypath
    rewrite:
      uri: /
    route:
    - destination:
        host: nginx
  - route:
    - destination:
        host: nginx
```

And then apply the change:

```
$ kubectl apply -f virtualservice.yaml
```

The updated virtual service includes a `match` attribute, which will look for the legacy path and rewrite it to simply target the root endpoint.

Now, calls to the legacy path from the `curl` pod will no longer produce a 404, but a 200 OK instead:

```
$ curl -v nginx/legacypath
*   Trying 10.152.183.90:80...
* Connected to nginx (10.152.183.90) port 80 (#0)
> GET /legacypath HTTP/1.1
> Host: nginx
> User-Agent: curl/8.1.2
> Accept: */*
>
< HTTP/1.1 200 OK
```

Discussion

The role of virtual services is mainly to define the routing from clients to upstream services. For additional control over the requests to the upstream service, refer to the Istio documentation on destination rules (*https://oreil.ly/Yu4xW*).

See Also

- Istio `HTTPRewrite` documentation (*https://oreil.ly/EGAFs*)

13.5 Installing the Linkerd Service Mesh

Problem

Your project requires a small footprint and/or doesn't need all the features provided by Istio, such as support for non-Kubernetes workloads or native support for egress.

Solution

You might be interested in trying Linkerd, which positions itself as a more lightweight alternative to Istio.

First, if you're directly following on from the Istio recipes, you can reset your environment by using a command like `kubectl delete all --all` (beware, this will remove *everything* from your cluster!).

You can then manually install Linkerd by executing the following command and following the instructions in the terminal:

```
$ curl --proto '=https' --tlsv1.2 -sSfL https://run.linkerd.io/install | sh
```

The output of the previous command will include additional steps, including updating your `PATH` as well as other checks and installation commands that are essential to completing the installation of Linkerd. The following snippet shows these instructions at time of writing:

```
...
Add the linkerd CLI to your path with:

  export PATH=$PATH:/Users/jonathanmichaux/.linkerd2/bin

Now run:

  linkerd check --pre                    # validate that Linkerd can be inst...
  linkerd install --crds | kubectl apply -f - # install the Linkerd CRDs
  linkerd install | kubectl apply -f -   # install the control plane into the...
  linkerd check                          # validate everything worked!
...
```

When you run the second of these `install` commands, you may get an error message recommending that you rerun that command with an additional parameter, as shown here:

```
linkerd install --set proxyInit.runAsRoot=true | kubectl apply -f -
```

At the end of the installation, you'll be asked to run a command that checks that everything is up and running correctly:

```
$ linkerd check
...
linkerd-control-plane-proxy
--------------------------
√ control plane proxies are healthy
√ control plane proxies are up-to-date
√ control plane proxies and cli versions match

Status check results are √
```

You should also be able to see the Linkerd pods running in the linkerd namespace:

```
$ kubectl get pods -n linkerd
NAME                                       READY   STATUS    RESTARTS   AGE
linkerd-destination-6b8c559b89-rx8f7       4/4     Running   0          9m23s
linkerd-identity-6dd765fb74-52plg          2/2     Running   0          9m23s
linkerd-proxy-injector-f54b7f688-lhjg6     2/2     Running   0          9m22s
```

Make sure Linkerd is configured to automatically inject the Linkerd proxy to services that you deploy. You can enable this for the default namespace with the following command:

```
$ kubectl annotate namespace default linkerd.io/inject=enabled
namespace/default annotate
```

Discussion

William Morgan, the cofounder and CEO of Buoyant Inc., was the first to coin the term *service mesh* in 2016. Since then, the community behind Bouyant's Linkerd has maintained its focus on providing a well-scoped, performant product.

As mentioned in the problem statement, one of the main limitations of Linkerd to be aware of, at time of writing, is that it can only mesh services that are running on Kubernetes.

See Also

- The Linkerd official Getting Started guide (*https://oreil.ly/zx-Wx*)

13.6 Deploying a Service into the Linkerd Mesh

Problem

You want to deploy a service into the Linkerd mesh and inject a sidecar into its pod.

Solution

Let's deploy the same `nginx` service as we did with Istio, which responds to HTTP GET requests on its root endpoint, returns a 404 response on others.

Start by creating a deployment for NGINX:

```
$ kubectl create deployment nginx --image nginx:1.25.2
deployment.apps/nginx created
```

Then expose this as a Kubernetes service:

```
$ kubectl expose deploy/nginx --port 80
service/nginx exposed
```

Now list the pods in the default namespace. You should have two containers in the `nginx` service's pod:

```
$ kubectl get po
NAME                     READY   STATUS    RESTARTS   AGE
nginx-748c667d99-fjjm4   2/2     Running   0          13s
```

If you investigate the details of this pod, you'll find that two Linkerd containers were injected into the pod. One is the init container, which plays a role in routing TCP traffic to and from the pod and which terminates before the other pods are started. The other container is the Linkerd proxy itself:

```
$ kubectl describe pod -l app=nginx | grep Image:
    Image:          cr.l5d.io/linkerd/proxy-init:v2.2.1
    Image:          cr.l5d.io/linkerd/proxy:stable-2.13.5
    Image:          nginx
```

Discussion

Like Istio, Linkerd relies on a sidecar proxy, also known as an ambassador container (*https://oreil.ly/ooN52*), that is injected into pods and provides additional functionality to the service running alongside it.

The Linkerd CLI provides the `linkerd inject` command as a useful alternative way to decide where and when to inject the Linkerd proxy container into the application pod, without manipulating labels yourself. You can read about it in the Linkerd documentation (*https://oreil.ly/KJfxJ*).

See Also

- More information on how to configure automatic sidecar injection (*https://oreil.ly/TexFs*)
- More information on the architecture of Linkerd (*https://oreil.ly/nTiTn*)

13.7 Routing Traffic to a Service in Linkerd

Problem

You want to deploy a service into the mesh that will invoke the `nginx` service you deployed in the previous recipe, and verify that Linkerd and its sidecars are intercepting and routing the traffic.

Solution

We'll simulate interservice communication within the service mesh by deploying a `curl` pod that will be added to the mesh and invoke the `nginx` service. As you'll see in this recipe, routing policies are defined differently in Linkerd.

First, run a `curl` pod that you'll use to invoke the service. Because you're starting the `curl` pod in the default namespace and you've activated automatic sidecar injection in this namespace (Recipe 13.5), the `curl` pod will automatically get a sidecar and be added to the mesh:

```
$ kubectl run mycurlpod --image=curlimages/curl -i --tty -- sh
Defaulted container "linkerd-proxy" out of: linkerd-proxy, mycurlpod,
linkerd-init (init)
error: Unable to use a TTY - container linkerd-proxy did not allocate one
If you don't see a command prompt, try pressing enter.
```

Because Linkerd modifies the default container ordering in a meshed pod, the previous `run` command will fail because it tries to tty into the Linkerd proxy, rather than our `curl` container.

To bypass this issue, you can unblock the terminal with CTRL-C and then run a command to connect into the correct container by using the `-c` flag:

```
$ kubectl attach mycurlpod -c mycurlpod -i -t
```

Now you can invoke the `nginx` service from the `curl` pod:

```
$ curl -v nginx
*   Trying 10.111.17.127:80...
* Connected to nginx (10.111.17.127) port 80 (#0)
> GET / HTTP/1.1
> Host: nginx
> User-Agent: curl/8.1.2
> Accept: */*
>
< HTTP/1.1 200 OK
< server: nginx/1.25.1
...
<
```

```
<!DOCTYPE html>
<html>
<head>
<title>Welcome to nginx!</title>
...
```

 You'll see the response from the nginx service, but unlike with Istio, there aren't yet any clear indicators that Linkerd has successfully intercepted this request.

To start adding a Linkerd routing policy to the nginx service, define a Linkerd Server resource in a file called *linkerd-server.yaml*, shown here:

```
apiVersion: policy.linkerd.io/v1beta1
kind: Server
metadata:
  name: nginx
  labels:
    app: nginx
spec:
  podSelector:
    matchLabels:
        app: nginx
  port: 80
```

Then create the server:

```
$ kubectl apply -f linkerd-server.yaml
server.policy.linkerd.io/nginx created
```

Now if you invoke the service again from the curl pod, you'll get confirmation that Linkerd is intercepting this request, because by default it will reject requests to servers that don't have an associated authorization policy:

```
$ curl -v nginx
*   Trying 10.111.17.127:80...
* Connected to nginx (10.111.17.127) port 80 (#0)
> GET / HTTP/1.1
> Host: nginx
> User-Agent: curl/8.1.2
> Accept: */*
>
< HTTP/1.1 403 Forbidden
< l5d-proxy-error: client 10.244.0.24:53274: server: 10.244.0.23:80:
unauthorized request on route
< date: Wed, 05 Jul 2023 20:33:24 GMT
< content-length: 0
<
```

Discussion

As you can see, Linkerd uses pod selector labels to determine which pods are governed by the policies of the mesh. In comparison, Istio's `VirtualService` resource references a service by name directly.

13.8 Authorizing Traffic to the Server in Linkerd

Problem

You've added a service like `nginx` to the mesh and declared it as a Linkerd server, but now you're getting 403 Forbidden responses because the mesh requires authorization by default on all declared servers.

Solution

Linkerd provides different policies to define which clients are allowed to contact which servers. In this example, we'll use a Linkerd `AuthorizationPolicy` to specify which service accounts can call the `nginx` service.

In your development environment, the `curl` pod is using the `default` service account, unless otherwise specified. In production, your services would have their own dedicated service accounts.

Start by creating a file called *linkerd-auth-policy.yaml*, as shown here:

```
apiVersion: policy.linkerd.io/v1alpha1
kind: AuthorizationPolicy
metadata:
  name: nginx-policy
spec:
  targetRef:
    group: policy.linkerd.io
    kind: Server
    name: nginx
  requiredAuthenticationRefs:
    - name: default
      kind: ServiceAccount
```

This policy declares that any client using the `default` service account will be able to access the Linkerd server called `nginx` that you created in the previous recipe.

Apply the policy:

```
$ kubectl apply -f linkerd-auth-policy.yaml
authorizationpolicy.policy.linkerd.io/nginx-policy created
```

Now you can invoke the `nginx` service from the `curl` pod and get a 200 OK:

```
$ curl -v nginx
*   Trying 10.111.17.127:80...
* Connected to nginx (10.111.17.127) port 80 (#0)
> GET / HTTP/1.1
> Host: nginx
> User-Agent: curl/8.1.2
> Accept: */*
>
< HTTP/1.1 200 OK
...
<!DOCTYPE html>
<html>
<head>
<title>Welcome to nginx!</title>
```

Discussion

Alternative ways to control access to servers include TLS identity-based policies, IP-based policies, specifically referencing clients by using pod selectors, and any combination of these.

Furthermore, default policies (*https://oreil.ly/LwiQ_*) can be applied that restrict access to services that aren't formally referenced by a Linkerd `Server` resource.

See Also

- Linkerd authorization policy documentation (*https://oreil.ly/FOtW1*)

## CHAPTER 14

Serverless and Event-Driven Applications

Serverless represents a cloud native paradigm for development, empowering developers to create and deploy applications without the burden of server management. While servers are still part of the equation, the platform abstracts them away from the intricacies of application development.

In this chapter, you will find recipes that show you how to deploy serverless workloads on Kubernetes using the Knative (*https://knative.dev*) stack.

14.1 Installing the Knative Operator

Problem

You want to deploy the Knative platform to your cluster.

Solution

Using the Knative Operator (*https://oreil.ly/y_7fy*), you can easily deploy the Knative stack components to your cluster. The operator defines custom resources (CRs), enabling you to easily configure, install, upgrade, and manage the lifecycle of the Knative stack.

To install version 1.11.4 of the Knative Operator from the release page (*https://oreil.ly/6CRLJ*), do this:

```
$ kubectl apply -f https://github.com/knative/operator/releases/download/
knative-v1.11.4/operator.yaml
```

Verify that the operator is running:

```
$ kubectl get deployment knative-operator
NAME               READY   UP-TO-DATE   AVAILABLE   AGE
knative-operator   1/1     1            1           13s
```

Discussion

Knative is an open source project that develops components for deploying, running, and managing serverless, cloud native applications on Kubernetes. The platform consists of two main components, namely Serving (*https://oreil.ly/dpMyf*) and Eventing (*https://oreil.ly/kYtPu*).

While the Knative Operator is the preferred method for deploying and configuring the Knative components, alternatively these components can be deployed using YAML files made available on their respective release pages.

14.2 Installing the Knative Serving Component

Problem

You've installed the Knative Operator (see Recipe 14.1), and now you want to deploy the Knative Serving (*https://oreil.ly/dpMyf*) component to run serverless applications.

Solution

Use the KnativeServing (*https://oreil.ly/v-LsX*) custom resource provided by the Knative Operator to install the Serving component of Knative.

Knative Serving should be installed in a namespace named knative-serving:

```
$ kubectl create ns knative-serving
namespace/knative-serving created
```

You must create a KnativeServing CR, add a networking layer, and configure the DNS. For the networking layer, we will use Kourier (*https://oreil.ly/5DRRi*), which is a lightweight Ingress object for Knative Serving. For the DNS, we will use the sslip.io (*https://sslip.io*) DNS service.

Create a file named *serving.yaml* with the following contents:

```
apiVersion: operator.knative.dev/v1beta1
kind: KnativeServing
metadata:
  name: knative-serving
  namespace: knative-serving
spec:
  ingress:
    kourier:
```

```
      enabled: true
  config:
    network:
      ingress-class: "kourier.ingress.networking.knative.dev"
```

Now use kubectl to apply this configuration:

```
$ kubectl apply -f serving.yaml
knativeserving.operator.knative.dev/knative-serving created
```

It will take a few minutes for the Knative Serving component to be successfully deployed. You can watch its deployment status using this:

```
$ kubectl -n knative-serving get KnativeServing knative-serving -w
NAME              VERSION   READY   REASON
knative-serving   1.11.0    False   NotReady
knative-serving   1.11.0    False   NotReady
knative-serving   1.11.0    True
```

Alternatively, you can install Knative Serving using YAML files:

```
$ kubectl apply -f https://github.com/knative/serving/releases/download/
knative-v1.11.0/serving-crds.yaml
$ kubectl apply -f https://github.com/knative/serving/releases/download/
knative-v1.11.0/serving-core.yaml
```

Check if the kourier service has been assigned an external IP address or CNAME:

```
$ kubectl -n knative-serving get service kourier
NAME      TYPE           CLUSTER-IP     EXTERNAL-IP    PORT(S)       AGE
kourier   LoadBalancer   10.99.62.226   10.99.62.226   80:30227/T... 118s
```

On a Minikube cluster, run the command minikube tunnel in a terminal so that the kourier service is assigned an external IP address.

Finally, configure Knative Serving to use sslip.io as the DNS suffix:

```
$ kubectl apply -f https://github.com/knative/serving/releases/download/
knative-v1.11.0/serving-default-domain.yaml
job.batch/default-domain created
service/default-domain-service created
```

Discussion

The Knative Serving component enables the Serving API. It provides a high-level abstraction for deploying, managing, and autoscaling serverless workloads, primarily focusing on stateless, request-driven applications. It aims to simplify the process of deploying and managing containerized applications in a serverless manner, allowing developers to focus on writing code without the need to manage infrastructure concerns.

sslip.io is a DNS service that allows you to easily access your applications deployed on Knative using domain names, without having to manage DNS records. The service URLs will have the sslip.io suffix and when queried with a hostname with an embedded IP address, the service will rturn that IP address.

In production environments, it is highly recommended that you configure a real DNS (*https://oreil.ly/Shtsq*) for workloads deployed on Knative.

See Also

- Installing Knative (*https://knative.dev/docs/install*)
- Configuring DNS (*https://oreil.ly/Shtsq*)

14.3 Installing the Knative CLI

Problem

You've installed the Knative Operator (Recipe 14.1), and now you want an easy way for managing Knative resources instead of dealing with YAML files.

Solution

Use kn (*https://knative.dev/docs/client/install-kn*), the Knative CLI.

Install the kn binary from the GitHub release page (*https://oreil.ly/wZXg6*) and move it into your $PATH. For example, to install kn v1.8.2 on macOS (Intel), do this:

```
$ wget https://github.com/knative/client/releases/download/knative-v1.11.0/
kn-darwin-amd64
```

```
$ sudo install -m 755 kn-darwin-amd64 /usr/local/bin/kn
```

Alternatively, Linux and macOS users can install the Knative CLI using the Homebrew (*https://brew.sh*) package manager:

```
$ brew install knative/client/kn
```

Installation of kn is extensively documented at the project page (*https://oreil.ly/Ks0Oh*).

Discussion

kn provides a quick and easy way of creating Knative resources such as services and event sources, without having to deal with YAML files directly. The kn tool provides a number of commands to manage Knative resources.

For an overview of the available commands, do this:

```
$ kn help
kn is the command line interface for managing Knative Serving and Eventing

Find more information about Knative at: https://knative.dev

Serving Commands:
  service     Manage Knative services
  revision    Manage service revisions
  ...

Eventing Commands:
  source      Manage event sources
  broker      Manage message brokers
  ...

Other Commands:
  plugin      Manage kn plugins
  completion  Output shell completion code
  version     Show the version of this client
```

You will find example usage scenarios of kn in the remainder of this chapter.

14.4 Creating a Knative Service

Problem

You've installed Knative Serving (see Recipe 14.2) and now want to deploy an application on Kubernetes that will release the cluster resources when not in use.

Solution

Use the Knative Serving API to create a Knative Service that automatically scales down to zero when not in use.

As an example, let's deploy the application functions/nodeinfo, which provides information about the Kubernetes node it's running on. Create a file named *nodeinfo.yaml* to deploy the application as a Knative Service:

```
apiVersion: serving.knative.dev/v1
kind: Service
metadata:
  name: nodeinfo
```

```
spec:
  template:
    spec:
      containers:
        - image: functions/nodeinfo:latest
```

It's important to note that this type of service is not the same as the `Service` object described in Figure 5-1; rather, this `Service` object is instantiated from the Knative Serving API (*https://oreil.ly/G3_jU*).

Deploy the application with this:

```
$ kubectl apply -f nodeinfo.yaml
service.serving.knative.dev/nodeinfo created
```

Check the status of the service with this:

```
$ kubectl get ksvc nodeinfo
NAME       URL                        LATESTCREATED   LATESTREADY     READY
nodeinfo   http://nodeinfo...sslip.io nodeinfo-00001  nodeinfo-00001  True
```

After the service has started successfully, open the URL in your browser to see the node information.

Now, take a look at the pods that were created for the service:

```
$ kubectl get po -l serving.knative.dev/service=nodeinfo -w
NAME                     READY   STATUS            RESTARTS   AGE
nodeinfo-00001-deploy... 0/2     Pending           0          0s
nodeinfo-00001-deploy... 0/2     Pending           0          0s
nodeinfo-00001-deploy... 0/2     ContainerCreating 0          0s
nodeinfo-00001-deploy... 1/2     Running           0          2s
nodeinfo-00001-deploy... 2/2     Running           0          2s
```

Close the browser window, and after about two minutes you should notice that the `nodeinfo` pods are automatically scaled down to zero:

```
$ kubectl get po -l serving.knative.dev/service=nodeinfo
No resources found in default namespace.
```

Now, if you open the URL in the browser, a new `Pod` object will automatically be started to handle the incoming request. You should notice a delay in rendering the page since a new `Pod` is created to handle this request.

Discussion

Using the kn client (see Recipe 14.3), you can create the service without having to write YAML files:

```
$ kn service create nodeinfo --image functions/nodeinfo:latest --port 8080
Creating service 'nodeinfo' in namespace 'default':

  0.054s The Route is still working to reflect the latest desired specification.
```

```
0.068s Configuration "nodeinfo" is waiting for a Revision to become ready.
3.345s ...
3.399s Ingress has not yet been reconciled.
3.481s Waiting for load balancer to be ready
3.668s Ready to serve.

Service 'nodeinfo' created to latest revision 'nodeinfo-00001' is available at
URL: http://nodeinfo.default.10.96.170.166.sslip.io
```

14.5 Installing the Knative Eventing Component

Problem

You've installed the Knative Operator (see Recipe 14.1), and now you want to
deploy the Knative Eventing (*https://oreil.ly/kYtPu*) component to build event-driven
applications.

Solution

Use the KnativeEventing (*https://oreil.ly/1u62U*) custom resource provided by the
Knative Operator to install the Eventing component of Knative.

Knative Eventing should be installed in a namespace named knative-eventing:

```
$ kubectl create ns knative-eventing
namespace/knative-eventing created
```

Create a file named *eventing.yaml* with the following contents:

```
apiVersion: operator.knative.dev/v1beta1
kind: KnativeEventing
metadata:
  name: knative-eventing
  namespace: knative-eventing
```

Now use kubectl to apply this configuration:

```
$ kubectl apply -f eventing.yaml
knativeeventing.operator.knative.dev/knative-eventing created
```

It will take a few minutes for the Knative Eventing component to be successfully
deployed. You can watch its deployment status using this:

```
$ kubectl --namespace knative-eventing get KnativeEventing knative-eventing -w
NAME              VERSION   READY   REASON
knative-eventing  1.11.1    False   NotReady
knative-eventing  1.11.1    False   NotReady
knative-eventing  1.11.1    False   NotReady
knative-eventing  1.11.1    True
```

Alternatively, to install Knative Eventing using YAML files, do this:

```
$ kubectl apply -f https://github.com/knative/eventing/releases/download/
knative-v1.11.1/eventing-crds.yaml
$ kubectl apply -f https://github.com/knative/eventing/releases/download/
knative-v1.11.1/eventing-core.yaml
```

And then install the in-memory channel and MTChannelBasedBroker:

```
$ kubectl apply -f https://github.com/knative/eventing/releases/download/
knative-v1.11.1/in-memory-channel.yaml
$ kubectl apply -f https://github.com/knative/eventing/releases/download/
knative-v1.11.1/mt-channel-broker.yaml
```

Discussion

The Knative Eventing component enables the Eventing API. It provides a framework for managing and handing events within a cloud native environment. Events in this context refer to occurrences or changes within a system, such as the creation of a new resource, updates to existing resources, or external triggers. This component enables developers to build reactive and flexible applications that respond to real-time changes and triggers across the cloud native ecosystem.

14.6 Deploying a Knative Eventing Source

Problem

You've installed Knative Eventing (see Recipe 14.5), and now you want to deploy a source that produces events so that you can use those events to trigger workflows in Knative.

Solution

An event source is a Kubernetes custom resource that acts as a link between an event producer and an event sink. To inspect the event sources currently available, do this:

```
$ kubectl api-resources --api-group='sources.knative.dev'
NAME               SHORTNAMES   APIVERSION          NAMESPACED   KIND
apiserversources                sources.kn...dev/v1  true        ApiServerSource
containersources                sources.kn...dev/v1  true        ContainerSource
pingsources                     sources.kn...dev/v1  true        PingSource
sinkbindings                    sources.kn...dev/v1  true        SinkBinding
```

PingSource (*https://oreil.ly/KlpSU*) is an event source that generates events containing a fixed payload at regular intervals defined by a cron schedule. Let's deploy a Ping Source and hook it on to a Sink (*https://oreil.ly/RWa85*) named sockeye.

Begin by creating the sockeye service:

```
$ kubectl apply -f https://github.com/n3wscott/sockeye/releases/download/
v0.7.0/release.yaml
service.serving.knative.dev/sockeye created
```

Verify that the sockeye service was created successfully:

```
$ kubectl get ksvc sockeye
NAME      URL                      LATESTCREATED   LATESTREADY    READY
sockeye   http://sockeye...sslip.io   sockeye-00001   sockeye-00001   True
```

Create a file named *pingsource.yaml* to create the PingSource and hook it up with the sockeye application:

```
apiVersion: sources.knative.dev/v1
kind: PingSource
metadata:
  name: ping-source
spec:
  schedule: "* * * * *"
  contentType: "application/json"
  data: '{ "message": "Hello, world!" }'
  sink:
    ref:
      apiVersion: serving.knative.dev/v1
      kind: Service
      name: sockeye
```

Apply the manifest with this:

```
$ kubectl apply -f pingsource.yaml
pingsource.sources.knative.dev/ping-source created
```

Verify that the PingSource was created successfully:

```
$ kubectl get pingsource ping-source -w
NAME          ...   AGE   READY   REASON
ping-source   ...   52s   False   MinimumReplicasUnavailable
ping-source   ...   59s   True
```

Get the URL of the sockeye service using this:

```
$ kubectl get ksvc sockeye  -o jsonpath={.status.url}
http://sockeye.default.10.99.62.226.sslip.io
```

Upon opening the URL in your web browser, you should see new events appear every minute, as shown in Figure 14-1.

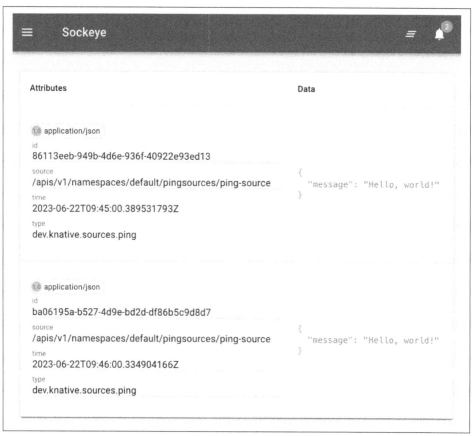

Figure 14-1. Events appearing in Sockeye

Discussion

If you do not want to write YAML files, you can use the kn client (see Recipe 14.3) instead.

Create the sockeye service with this:

```
$ kn service create sockeye --image docker.io/n3wscott/sockeye:v0.7.0
```

Next, create the PingSource:

```
$ kn source ping create ping-source --data '{ "message": "Hello, world!" }' \
    --schedule '* * * * *' --sink sockeye
```

14.7 Enabling Knative Eventing Sources

Problem

You've installed the Knative Eventing component (see Recipe 14.5), and you want to enable Knative event sources that are not enabled by default.

Solution

Additional event sources (*https://oreil.ly/ZP2Wa*) developed by the Knative community, such as ones for GitHub, GitLab, Apache Kafka, and so on, can be configured in the Knative Eventing custom resource. For instance, to install the GitHub event source (*https://oreil.ly/8HavC*), update the *eventing.yaml* file from Recipe 14.5 like so:

```
apiVersion: operator.knative.dev/v1beta1
kind: KnativeEventing
metadata:
  name: knative-eventing
  namespace: knative-eventing
spec:
  source:
    github:
      enabled: true
```

Apply the changes with this:

```
$ kubectl apply -f eventing.yaml
knativeeventing.operator.knative.dev/knative-eventing configured
```

Watch the status of the update:

```
$ kubectl -n knative-eventing get KnativeEventing knative-eventing -w
NAME              VERSION   READY   REASON
knative-eventing  1.11.1    False   NotReady
knative-eventing  1.11.1    True
```

Now, if you inspect the available sources, you should see the `GitHubSource` event source:

```
$ kubectl api-resources --api-group='sources.knative.dev'
NAME              APIVERSION             NAMESPACED   KIND
apiserversources  sources.kn..dev/v1     true         ApiServerSource
containersources  sources.kn..dev/v1     true         ContainerSource
githubsources     sources.kn..dev/v1alpha1   true     GitHubSource
pingsources       sources.kn..dev/v1     true         PingSource
sinkbindings      sources.kn..dev/v1     true         SinkBinding
```

Discussion

The `GitHubSource` event source registers for events on a specified GitHub organization or repository and triggers a new event for selected GitHub event types.

Open source event sources for GitLab, Apache Kafka, RabbitMQ, and more are also available.

14.8 Installing Event Sources from TriggerMesh

Problem

You've installed Knative Eventing (see Recipe 14.5), and now you want to install event sources from TriggerMesh so that you have access to event sources for a wide range of platforms and services.

Solution

To install v1.26.0 of TriggerMesh, do this:

```
$ kubectl apply -f https://github.com/triggermesh/triggermesh/releases/
download/v1.26.0/triggermesh-crds.yaml
...k8s.io/awscloudwatchlogssources.sources.triggermesh.io created
...k8s.io/awscloudwatchsources.sources.triggermesh.io created
...k8s.io/awscodecommitsources.sources.triggermesh.io create
...
```

```
$ kubectl apply -f https://github.com/triggermesh/triggermesh/releases/
download/v1.26.0/triggermesh.yaml
namespace/triggermesh created
clusterrole.rbac.authorization.k8s.io/triggermesh-namespaced-admin created
clusterrole.rbac.authorization.k8s.io/triggermesh-namespaced-edit created
clusterrole.rbac.authorization.k8s.io/triggermesh-namespaced-view created
...
```

You can inspect the sources provided by the TriggerMesh API using this:

```
$ kubectl api-resources --api-group='sources.triggermesh.io'
NAME                   APIVERSION        NAMESPACED  KIND
awscloudwatchlog...    sources.tri...    true        AWSCloudWatchLogsSource
awscloudwatchsou...    sources.tri...    true        AWSCloudWatchSource
awscodecommitsou...    sources.tri...    true        AWSCodeCommitSource
...
```

Similarly, you can list all the sinks provided by the TriggerMesh API using this:

```
$ kubectl api-resources --api-group='targets.triggermesh.io'
NAME                 SHORT...  APIVERSION      NAMESPACED  KIND
awscomprehendtar...            targets.tri...  true        AWSComprehendTarget
awsdynamodbtarge...            targets.tri...  true        AWSDynamoDBTarget
awseventbridgeta...            targets.tri...  true        AWSEventBridgeTarget
...
```

Discussion

TriggerMesh (*https://triggermesh.com*) is free open source software that lets you easily build event-driven applications. TriggerMesh provides event sources for a wide range of platforms and services, such as AWS, Google Cloud, Azure, Salesforce, Zendesk, and so on. In addition to event sources, TriggerMesh provides components that enable you to transform the cloud events.

Head over to the TriggerMesh documentation (*https://oreil.ly/0lDap*) to learn more.

See Also

- TriggerMesh sources (*https://oreil.ly/-bqVQ*)
- TriggerMesh targets (*https://oreil.ly/7tlVP*)
- TriggerMesh transformations (*https://oreil.ly/O2Et4*)

## CHAPTER 15

Extending Kubernetes

Now that you've seen how to install, interact with, and use Kubernetes to deploy and manage applications, we focus in this chapter on adapting Kubernetes to your needs. For the recipes in this chapter, you will need Go (*https://go.dev*) installed and access to the Kubernetes source code hosted on GitHub (*https://github.com/kubernetes/kuber netes*). We show how to compile Kubernetes as a whole, and how to compile specific components like the client kubectl. We also demonstrate how to use Python to talk to the Kubernetes API server and show how to extend Kubernetes with a custom resource definition.

15.1 Compiling from Source

Problem

You want to build your own Kubernetes binaries from source instead of downloading the official release binaries (see Recipe 2.9) or third-party artifacts.

Solution

Clone the Kubernetes Git repository and build from source.

If your development machine has Docker Engine installed, you can use the quick-release target of the root *Makefile*, as shown here:

```
$ git clone https://github.com/kubernetes/kubernetes.git
$ cd kubernetes
$ make quick-release
```

This Docker-based build requires at least 8 GB of RAM to complete. Ensure that your Docker daemon has access to that much memory. On macOS, access the Docker for Mac preferences and increase the allocated RAM.

The binaries will be located in the _output/release-stage_ directory, and a complete bundle will be in the _output/release-tars_ directory.

Alternatively, if you have a Golang (*https://go.dev/doc/install*) environment properly set up, use the `release` target of the root *Makefile*:

```
$ git clone https://github.com/kubernetes/kubernetes.git
$ cd kubernetes
$ make
```

The binaries will be located in the _output/bin_ directory.

See Also

- The Kubernetes developer guides (*https://oreil.ly/6CSWo*)

15.2 Compiling a Specific Component

Problem

You want to build one specific component of Kubernetes from source. For example, you only want to build the client `kubectl`.

Solution

Instead of using `make quick-release` or simply `make`, as shown in Recipe 15.1, use `make kubectl`.

There are targets in the root *Makefile* to build individual components. For example, to compile `kubectl`, `kubeadm`, and `kubelet`, do this:

```
$ make kubectl kubeadm kubelet
```

The binaries will be located in the _output/bin_ directory.

 To get the complete list of *Makefile* build targets, run `make help`.

15.3 Using a Python Client to Interact with the Kubernetes API

Problem

As a developer, you want to use Python to write scripts that use the Kubernetes API.

Solution

Install the Python `kubernetes` module. This module (*https://oreil.ly/OolLt*) is the official Python client library for Kubernetes. You can install the module from source or from the Python Package Index (PyPi) site (*https://pypi.org*):

```
$ pip install kubernetes
```

With a Kubernetes cluster reachable using your default `kubectl` context, you are now ready to use this Python module to talk to the Kubernetes API. For example, the following Python script lists all the pods and prints their names:

```
from kubernetes import client, config

config.load_kube_config()

v1 = client.CoreV1Api()
res = v1.list_pod_for_all_namespaces(watch=False)
for pod in res.items:
    print(pod.metadata.name)
```

The `config.load_kube_config()` call in this script will load your Kubernetes credentials and endpoint from your `kubectl` config file. By default, it will load the cluster endpoint and credentials for your current context.

Discussion

The Python client is built using the OpenAPI specification of the Kubernetes API. It is up to date and autogenerated. All APIs are available through this client.

Each API group corresponds to a specific class, so to call a method on an API object that is part of the `/api/v1` API group, you need to instantiate the `CoreV1Api` class. To use deployments, you will need to instantiate the `extensionsV1beta1Api` class. All methods and corresponding API group instances can be found in the autogenerated *README* (*https://oreil.ly/ITREP*).

See Also

- Examples in the project's repository (*https://oreil.ly/6rw3l*)

15.4 Extending the API Using Custom Resource Definitions

Problem

You have a custom workload and none of the existing resources, such as Deployment, Job, or StatefulSet, is a good fit. So, you want to extend the Kubernetes API with a new resource that represents your workload while continuing to use kubectl in the usual way.

Solution

Use a custom resource definition (CRD) (*https://oreil.ly/d2MmH*).

Let's say you want to define a custom resource of kind Function. This represents a short-running Job-like kind of resource, akin to what AWS Lambda offers, that is a function as a service (FaaS, or sometimes misleadingly called a "serverless function").

For a production-ready FaaS solution running on Kubernetes, see Chapter 14.

First, define the CRD in a manifest file called *functions-crd.yaml*:

```
apiVersion: apiextensions.k8s.io/v1
kind: CustomResourceDefinition
metadata:
  name: functions.example.com
spec:
  group: example.com
  versions:
  - name: v1
    served: true
    storage: true
    schema:
      openAPIV3Schema:
        type: object
        properties:
          spec:
            type: object
            properties:
              code:
                type: string
              ram:
                type: string
  scope:            Namespaced
  names:
    plural: functions
```

```
    singular: function
    kind: Function
```

Then let the API server know about your new CRD (it can take several minutes to register):

```
$ kubectl apply -f functions-crd.yaml
customresourcedefinition.apiextensions.k8s.io/functions.example.com created
```

Now that you have the custom resource Function defined and the API server knows about it, you can instantiate it using a manifest called *myfaas.yaml* with the following contents:

```
apiVersion: example.com/v1
kind: Function
metadata:
  name: myfaas
spec:
  code: "http://src.example.com/myfaas.js"
  ram: 100Mi
```

And create the myfaas resource of kind Function as per usual:

```
$ kubectl apply -f myfaas.yaml
function.example.com/myfaas created
```

```
$ kubectl get crd functions.example.com -o yaml
apiVersion: apiextensions.k8s.io/v1
kind: CustomResourceDefinition
metadata:
  creationTimestamp: "2023-05-02T12:12:03Z"
  generation: 1
  name: functions.example.com
  resourceVersion: "2494492251"
  uid: 5e0128b3-95d9-412b-b84d-b3fac030be75
spec:
  conversion:
    strategy: None
  group: example.com
  names:
    kind: Function
    listKind: FunctionList
    plural: functions
    shortNames:
    - fn
    singular: function
  scope: Namespaced
  versions:
  - name: v1
    schema:
      openAPIV3Schema:
        properties:
          spec:
```

```
            properties:
              code:
                type: string
              ram:
                type: string
            type: object
          type: object
      served: true
      storage: true
  status:
    acceptedNames:
      kind: Function
      listKind: FunctionList
      plural: functions
      shortNames:
      - fn
      singular: function
    conditions:
    - lastTransitionTime: "2023-05-02T12:12:03Z"
      message: no conflicts found
      reason: NoConflicts
      status: "True"
      type: NamesAccepted
    - lastTransitionTime: "2023-05-02T12:12:03Z"
      message: the initial names have been accepted
      reason: InitialNamesAccepted
      status: "True"
      type: Established
    storedVersions:
    - v1

$ kubectl describe functions.example.com/myfaas
Name:         myfaas
Namespace:    triggermesh
Labels:       <none>
Annotations:  <none>
API Version:  example.com/v1
Kind:         Function
Metadata:
  Creation Timestamp:  2023-05-02T12:13:07Z
  Generation:          1
  Resource Version:    2494494012
  UID:                 bed83736-6c40-4039-97fb-2730c7a4447a
Spec:
  Code:  http://src.example.com/myfaas.js
  Ram:   100Mi
Events:  <none>
```

To discover CRDs, simply access the API server. For example, using kubectl proxy,
you can access the API server locally and query the key space (example.com/v1 in
our case):

```
$ curl 127.0.0.1:8001/apis/example.com/v1/ | jq .
{
  "kind": "APIResourceList",
  "apiVersion": "v1",
  "groupVersion": "example.com/v1",
  "resources": [
    {
      "name": "functions",
      "singularName": "function",
      "namespaced": true,
      "kind": "Function",
      "verbs": [
        "delete",
        "deletecollection",
        "get",
        "list",
        "patch",
        "create",
        "update",
        "watch"
      ],
      "shortNames": [
        "fn"
      ],
      "storageVersionHash": "FLWxvcx1j74="
    }
  ]
}
```

Here you can see the resource along with the allowed verbs.

When you want to get rid of your custom resource instance, simply delete it:

```
$ kubectl delete functions.example.com/myfaas
function.example.com "myfaas" deleted
```

Discussion

As you've seen, it is straightforward to create a CRD. From an end user's point of view, CRDs present a consistent API and are more or less indistinguishable from native resources such as pods or jobs. All the usual commands, such as kubectl get and kubectl delete, work as expected.

Creating a CRD is, however, really less than half of the work necessary to fully extend the Kubernetes API. On their own, CRDs only let you store and retrieve custom data via the API server in etcd. You need to also write a custom controller (*https://oreil.ly/kYmqw*) that interprets the custom data expressing the user's intent, establishes a control loop comparing the current state with the declared state, and tries to reconcile both.

See Also

- "Extend the Kubernetes API with `CustomResourceDefinitions`" (*https://oreil.ly/mz2bH*) in the Kubernetes documentation
- "Custom Resources" (*https://oreil.ly/gp0xn*) in the Kubernetes documentation

Resources

General

- Kubernetes documentation (*https://kubernetes.io/docs/home*)
- Kubernetes GitHub repository (*https://github.com/kubernetes/kubernetes*)
- Kubernetes GitHub community (*https://github.com/kubernetes/community*)
- Kubernetes Slack community (*https://slack.k8s.io*)

Tutorials and Examples

- Kube by Example (*https://kubebyexample.com*)
- Play with Kubernetes (*https://labs.play-with-k8s.com*)
- *Kubernetes: Up and Running*, Second Edition, by Brendan Burns, Joe Beda, and Kelsey Hightower (O'Reilly)

Index

About the Authors

Sameer Naik is a cloud native engineer with a background in embedded systems. He has been involved with various open source projects and was an early adopter of the Docker project. He is the author of several popular open source Docker application images. Sameer has been involved with the Kubernetes project from an early stage and is a founding member of the Helm Charts project. Sameer previously worked at VMware and Bitnami and is cofounder of NextBit Computing, an embedded systems start-up.

Sébastien Goasguen is a cofounder of TriggerMesh and a 20-year open source veteran. A member of the Apache Software Foundation, he worked on Apache CloudStack and Libcloud for several years before diving into the container world. Sébastien is also the founder of Skippbox, a Kubernetes start-up acquired by Bitnami. An avid blogger, he enjoys spreading the word about new cutting-edge technologies. Sébastien is the author of the O'Reilly *Docker Cookbook* and *60 Recipes for Apache CloudStack*.

Jonathan Michaux is a product manager, software engineer, and computer scientist, with a career spanning multiple start-ups and publicly traded companies. His mission has consistently revolved around delivering transformative tools for developers, including in the realms of API management, data and application integration, microservices, and most recently event-driven applications on Kubernetes. He holds a PhD in computer science, specializing in formal methods for concurrent systems.

Colophon

The animal on the cover of *Kubernetes Cookbook* is a Bengal eagle owl *(Bubo bengalensis)*. These large horned owls are usually seen in pairs and can be found in hilly and rocky scrub forests throughout South Asia.

The Bengal eagle owl measures 19–22 inches tall and weighs between 39–70 ounces. Its feathers are brownish-gray or beige, and its ears have brown tufts. In contrast to the neutral color of its body, its eye color is strikingly orange. Owls with orange eyes hunt during the day. It prefers a meaty diet and mostly feasts on rodents such as mice or rats but will also resort to eating other birds during the winter. This owl produces a deep, resonant, booming, two-note "whooo" call that can be heard at dusk and dawn.

Females build nests in shallow recesses in the ground, rock ledges, and riverbanks, and lay two to five cream-colored eggs. The eggs hatch after 33 days. By the time the chicks are around 10 weeks of age, they are adult-sized, though not mature yet, and they depend on their parents for nearly six months. To distract predators from their offspring, the parents will pretend to have a wing injury or fly in a zigzag manner.

Many of the animals on O'Reilly covers are endangered; all of them are important to the world.

The cover illustration is by Karen Montgomery, based on a black-and-white engraving from *Meyers Kleines Lexicon*. The cover fonts are Gilroy Semibold and Guardian Sans. The text font is Adobe Minion Pro; the heading font is Adobe Myriad Condensed; and the code font is Dalton Maag's Ubuntu Mono.

Milton Keynes UK
Ingram Content Group UK Ltd.
UKHW032046020124
435364UK00004B/10

9 781098 142247